What Now Skipper?

What Now Skipper?

Forty fiendish challenges to your seamanship skills

DES SLEIGHTHOLME, ANDREW BRAY,
TOM CUNLIFFE, BILL ANDERSON

SHERIDAN HOUSE

First published 1991 by
Sheridan House Inc.
145 Palisade Street
Dobbs Ferry, NY 10522

Charts reproduced on pp. 127, 139 by permission of the Hydrographer of
the Navy.

Printed in Great Britain

ISBN 0-924486-18-X

CONTENTS

PART THREE

INTRODUCTION

The airline pilot is lucky. Before being let loose on the controls of a Jumbo he will have had the benefit of long hours wrestling the controls of a flight simulator as the ground roars up to meet him and the instructor programmes the computer with a bewildering series of implausible accidents to test his skill. Alas, the same is not true for the yachtsman. The first time the wind starts howling in the rigging, the water rises hungrily in the bilge from a broken seacock, or the Decca bleeps its last, will be for real.

It is a strange fact about sailing that the situation with which you are faced is seldom exactly the one for which you have so carefully planned. Countless berthing manoeuvres will not have prepared you for that particular concoction of wind and tide, with a gearbox that mysteriously refuses to engage reverse. Man overboard practice is never accompanied by the complication of a mainsail that cannot be hoisted, a crew man rolling in the cockpit with blood pouring from a head wound and an engine *hors de combat* with a rope around the propeller.

The idea for this book came from a series of short articles in *Yachting Monthly* called 'Questions of Seamanship' in which an anonymous expert – probably one of the authors of this book – set readers fiendish little problems and supplied an answer later on. But what if, for a change, the experts were asked the questions – a sort of nautical Mastermind and no conferring? How would the Editor of *Yachting Monthly* and the Cruising Secretary of the RYA cope with the kind of problem they so often take delight in setting their readers or Yachtmaster pupils?

The answer lies in the following pages. Each author was asked to supply ten questions ranging from the everyday to the outlandish. Very few are real horror stories although most are tales of the unexpected. Reading between the lines many were culled from personal experience. Others were completely fictitious. Most had no simple answer. The questions were then shuffled and sent back to be answered. Finally the original questionmasters were given the chance to supply their own solutions and comment on the answers supplied by their co-authors.

Inevitably there were differences of approach and opinion. There can never be *an* answer to any question concerning the sea although the consensus among the four authors was remarkable. A few clues were missed here and there but by and large our experts acquitted themselves with distinction, providing a set of problems and attendant answers that are as ingenious as they are instructive.

With only tiny exceptions what appears here is what was originally written. By agreeing to put their reputations on the line so readily Andrew Bray (AB), Tom Cunliffe (TC), Des Sleightholme (JDS) and Bill Anderson (BA) proved that experience, allied to confidence is very nearly everything at sea.

Adrian Morgan
Editor Stanford Maritime

PART ONE

The only blemish on the idyllic scene was the shadow of the lee cap shroud . . .

Rig tension

Richard Symonds always looked forward to his annual cruise with Joe King with somewhat mixed feelings. Joe kept his boat in beautiful condition, the old wooden hull was as tight and as fair as the day she was first launched half a century ago. What worried Richard was Joe's unshakeable belief that his boat's longevity was due in large measure to the fact that none of her three owners had ever, as Joe put it 'Wound her up too tight on the bottlescrews'. Joe's fixation with the merits of slack shrouds seemed to get more fanatical as the years went by and any suggestion that a little tension might help to ensure that the mast continued to point skywards was treated with scorn and derision.

This year Richard's first impression as he grabbed the lower shroud to heave himself out of the dinghy encouraged him to suspect that Joe might have had a change of mind about his slack rigging policy. A surreptitious shove at the cap shroud soon dissillusioned him. Joe grinned at him from the dinghy.

'I saw that,' he said, 'don't you start nagging me about the rig. That old spar needs a bit of movement, it's been fine for 50 years but strap it up too tight and you'll snap it.'

'I'll remind you of those wise words when it goes over the side' Richard answered, outwardly smiling but inwardly wincing. He well knew that argument would be a waste of breath.

The two men had been sailing together for enough years to have achieved that happy relationship in which they needed to say very little to each other. In almost total silence they stowed their gear, shared a pot of tea, slipped the mooring and cleared the river. They had made for Breskens as the first leg of the summer cruise for as long as they could remember and all that needed to be said had been said many years ago. There was nothing resentful about their silence, it was bred of a shared love of peace and quiet, and a belief that the sound of the water against the hull made better listening than the clacking of tongues.

When Richard came on deck to take over the watch at midnight the boat was making a steady five knots on a close reach on port. The land was no longer in sight and there was little shipping around. It was a warm night and if it hadn't been for the odd splash of spray he would hardly have needed his oilskins. The only blemish on the idyllic scene was the shadow of the lee cap shroud cast on the mainsail by the moonlight. It seemed to be moving an alarming distance as the slack wire carved out an arc in response to the pitching of the boat.

Richard couldn't take his eyes off the dancing shadow on the sail. 'The middle of that shroud is moving at least three feet' he thought, 'that must be ten percent of it's length. That must be wrong, it can't be moving that much or it wouldn't hold the mast up.'

Suddenly he realised what was wrong with the shadow. He grabbed a torch, stood up and shone the beam at the leeward chain plates. Trailing from the top of the cap shroud bottlescrew was the spreader. It had dropped out of the socket on the mast and slid down the shroud, attached only by the anti-chafing pad on the outboard end.

Joe could not have been asleep because he was on deck within seconds in answer to Richard's shout. For a moment he thought that Richard was just having another nag about slack rigging but he very soon realised that this time there really was a problem.

It didn't take Joe long to decide on the solution to the problem. He grinned mischievously.

'Lucky you're lighter than me, old friend, so there's no doubt about who is going up in the bosun's chair. You shouldn't have any difficulty slipping the spreader back into the socket and I've got a couple of spare retaining pins in case you drop one. Good thing the shroud's not too tight or it would have been quite a struggle to slot it back in.'

Richard wasn't so sure. 'Wouldn't it be wiser just to drop the sails and motor home?' He asked. We could set up the main halyard to the chain plates to stop the head of the mast from whipping as she rolls.'

12

'We could,' answered Joe, 'If I hadn't forgotten to bring the spare can of fuel. I hoped I wouldn't have to admit this but we've only got a couple of hours worth in the tank and we must be at least 25 miles out by now.'

Richard still wasn't convinced. 'With a tight main halyard as a jury shroud I reckon we could at least carry a small jib on the other tack', he suggested.

Whose side are you on, or do you have a better idea than either of them?   BA

Heave to on port and try fixing that crosstree — trickier than it sounds. Failing this the taut halyard, but it would be no real substitute due to its narrow angle. Since they can apparently lay the course on a close reach they may not need to tack, but in an emergency drop sails and start engine, or at least deep reef the main and drop jib. I've tried working aloft at night, bad news.   IDS

I'm not too keen on Des's answer. It cannot be good seamanship to sail on with an untackable boat. What if they have to alter course for a group of fishing vessels? The options are going to be pretty limited. I would prefer the following.

Up the mast and replace the spreader. The only problem will be to keep the boat on course with no helmsman, but that should not be too difficult to solve with an over-sheeted jib and a lashed tiller. Heaving to on port would also be a possibility but a hove-to boat doesn't put as steady a load on her rig as one which is sailing. Any attempt to go back to harbour without replacing the spreader could be disastrous if there is a marked increase in wind and sea.

Replacing the spreader would be a great deal easier in daylight but I would resist the temptation to postpone his job. Until that spreader is replaced the boat is very limited in her freedom to manoeuvre and any deterioration in the weather is going to make the replacement much more difficult.   BA

Landfall

Brian Marshall heaved a sigh of relief. The slender column was now clearly visible on the starboard bow and it matched perfectly with the description of Barfleur Point Lighthouse in the Pilot. He had successfully completed his first Channel crossing; with the French Coast in sight and a mark positively identified his worries were over and he could relax.

'Keep her heading south' he said to his wife Maureen who was steering. 'The Pilot advises a good offing between the point and Barfleur harbour to keep clear of the off-lying rocks. I'm going to get a bearing for a running fix.'

Three quarters of an hour later he had a fix on the chart which showed that they were five miles off the harbour and approaching the leading line of 219 degrees. Pointe de Saire had now become clearly visible to the south but Brian had not yet managed to identify either the town or the harbour of Barfleur. The low afternoon sun was making it impossible to pick out any detail on the coast.

A two-bearing fix on Pointe de Barfleur and Pointe de Saire confirmed the earlier running fix. Brian asked Maureen to come close hauled and he hardened in on the sheets. The best they could manage was slightly to leeward of the course they needed so Brian started the engine and they stowed the sails.

'What's the course?' asked Maureen.

'Two one nine I think' Brian replied. 'But we've a problem. I can't see anything identifiable against the glare of the sun, so I'm not too happy about closing the coast.'

Maureen digested this information. 'Couldn't we edge in a bit closer?' she asked. 'Maybe we'll be able to see more as the sun gets round to the north of west and we can't afford to hang around, it's high water in half an hour and we only have enough water to get into the harbour until two hours after high.'

Brian looked unhappy. 'I don't think we should' he replied. 'My last fix is only two position lines and one of those was a rather vague edge of land down to the south. It's not just that I can't positively identify the coastal features ashore, there should be a buoy half a mile off the coast and I can't see that either.'

Maureen began to loose patience. 'Surely we could motor slowly in, keeping a close eye on the echosounder' she suggested.

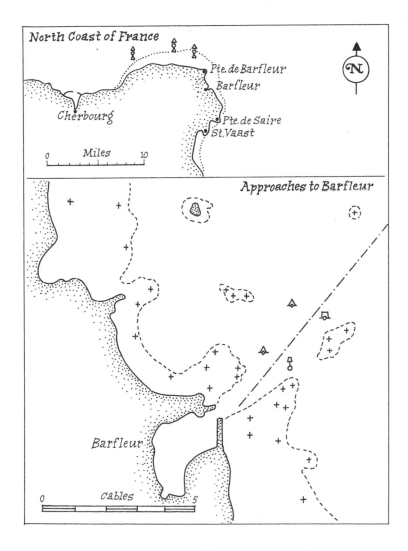

Brian wasn't convinced. 'I'd rather not' he said. 'In fact I think it might be better to give Barfleur a miss. The tide's fair for Cherbourg. I know it's to windward but it is a well-lit entrance and we could motor round there in eight hours. We could be off the entrance by 0300, get a positive identification on everything from the light characteristics and go in at dawn.'

Now it was Maureen's turn to look unhappy. She was looking forward to a large Armagnac in a harbour-side café, not a night motoring to windward.

Whose side are you on? Or do you have a better idea?　　BA

Brian is understandably cautious – a slightly uncertain landfall on a rocky coast at the end of his first Channel crossing – whilst Maureen quite rightly wants to get to the fleshpots to celebrate their successful passage. Although clearly marked, the entrance to Barfleur isn't easy and does seem a strange choice of destination for a first time crossing, the more so as the harbour dries. However, I am firmly with Maureen but with a slightly modified plan.

Brian shouldn't dismiss his two-point fix as it does tally with his earlier running fix which I assume he has worked accurately, making adequate provision for the strong tides that can run off Barfleur. And he is still five miles off so has little chance of picking out any of the offlying buoys. He should listen to Maureen and edge in on his course of 219 degrees, corrected for compass and tide. As the sun moves around so it will become easier to see both buoys and shore marks or, if he still fails to confirm his position, safe to haul off into deeper water before becoming enmeshed in any of the inshore dangers which extend up to a mile offshore. But really he's wasting his time.

Five miles or so further down the coast is a much more attractive destination, easier in the approaches, where he can stay afloat and where there is a far better choice of shoreside delights: St Vaast la Hogue. He still has an hour or so of fair stream – quite enough to see him down the coast – and as the lock gates stay open until three hours after HW he has plenty of time. St Vaast is also more easily identified from seaward and as he follows the coast along he'll have plenty of opportunity to fix his position accurately. And Maureen will be able to enjoy her Armagnac and congratulate herself for persuading Brian to change his plans. AB

I think Andrew is factually right about St Vaast but we cannot assume that Brian has local knowledge even acquired at second hand from someone familiar with this coast. I agree with his first paragraph and all except the last line of his second. My feeling is that the only problem is in the skipper's mind. He is right to be cautious, but that doesn't mean he must be over cautious. Leading marks which are invisible from four or five miles are not an uncommon phenomenon, particularly when looking directly up-sun. Close the land, navigating carefully and watching the echo sounder and all will be revealed. BA

Romeo and the sinking ship

'She'll do.' Curly looked up at his wife through the gaping engine room hatches. These were large openings which formed the major part of the sole of the centre cockpit on the 38ft ketch they had agreed to run 300 miles up the coast. Joanna was leaning over the coaming wearing an unsupported tee-shirt in the Mediterranean heat and Curly reminded himself that if ever the yacht delivery business collapsed, she'd be able to keep him by posing for the daily tabloids. For the time being, though, they were young, fit and having more fun by seeing the world, or at least the sea, as freelance yacht crew.

Curly's programme on a boat they didn't know always involved a thorough check on rig, engine and general watertight integrity. In the case of the current craft which was heavily built in grp, this latter had required nothing more than a look at all the seacocks and a turn with a screwdriver to test each hose clamp. Everything was in good order, which is what he expected, because the boat was only 18 months old and was a top-of-the-line production cruiser from a well respected British firm.

Curly's last job after inspecting the lubricating oil and battery acid levels was to ensure that the engine cooling water and the two cockpit drain seacocks were in the open position. He admired the way the armoured plastic hoses leading from the drain seacocks to the deep runnel surrounding the heavy cockpit sole hatches were cleverly routed without crossing the compartment so that they didn't get in his way as he climbed out of the engine room. He closed the hatches with a satisfying heavy 'clunk' and shot the securing bolts.

'All right?' enquired Joanna.

'We can't do more,' replied Curly. 'All we need now is a third hand. What a shame Alf let us down.' The boat despite her otherwise excellent equipment was suffering from a defective autopilot and neither Joanna nor her husband cared to steer for 12 hours out of 24.

'I've solved that one,' announced Joanna archly. 'While you were in the bilge, Alf swung by with a mate of his called Mario. He says he wants to come along. He's Italian and it seems he's been sailing since he was knee-high.'

'Yeah,' growled Curly, 'but has he ever been to sea?'

'I don't know,' she replied, 'but he's ever so keen. That's him sitting at the bar over there, making sheep's eyes at us.'

Curly squinted into the sun and took in the muscular form of the young man on the bar stool. His white shorts, which were hitched up to display bulging thighs, looked too clean for Curly's taste, but then Curly wasn't in a position to pick and choose, and the guy did at least look fit enough for the job. 'Oh well,' thought Curly, 'he might be a gigolo, but I've only got to put up with him for a couple of days.'

So off they went.

Twelve hours later it was pitch dark and blowing a full gale right on the nose. The boat was ten miles from land and hove-to on the offshore tack. Mario was crashed out in splendour down aft, Curly was off watch on the downhill saloon settee berth and Joanna was keeping an eye out for shipping from the cockpit. She had zipped up the windward dodgers and was reasonably dry, but there was something in the motion of the well-heeled boat that she didn't like, so she called down to Curly.

The skipper was exhausted after the pre-voyage preparations. He opened one eye, told her not to worry, and fell back into a deep sleep.

An hour later she woke him again. This time her voice was urgent. As Curly turned over to see what was happening, his arm fell over the side of the settee into elbow-deep water. This concentrated his mind wonderfully and in seconds he had vaulted up into the cockpit in his skivvies.

'Sorry about that,' he apologised coolly. 'You were right. We *are* sinking! You wake Mario and stick him on the aft pump, then start pumping up here yourself, and I'll find out what's going on.'

Almost literally, Curly dived below to begin his investigations and was soon aware of the pumps getting down to their rhythmic work. Mario's was operating faster than he'd ever heard a pump go before and he reflected that there was nothing like a terrified Latin for shifting water. But the pumps weren't winning. Soon Mario's voice came floating down to Curly who was inspecting the forward heads for the problem.

'I pumpa no more. Now I launcha the lifa-raft!'

'Like hell you do!' Joanna sounded like Queen Victoria caught in a vulgar moment. 'He'll tell you when to do that, in the meantime, get cracking!'

By the time Curly had worked his way to the forward bulkhead of the engine room he could hear water slopping into the boat from somewhere abaft his current location but before he could investigate Mario gave a cry of triumph.

'Is alright! We are saved! A ship. She is a-coming!'

'Coaster in sight, Curly.' Joanna reported down the hatch,

panting from her exertions at the pump. 'About two miles up to windward, going up the coast.'

As Curly turned to respond, Mario's face appeared by the side of Joanna's. His eyes were white in the torch beam and his nostrils were flaring.

'Now you maka the Mayday!' He shrieked. 'I pumpa no more.'

Curly looked at Mario's panic-stricken expression. Then he shifted his gaze to Joanna; calm but anxious. Every time the yacht was pressed down to leeward by a passing wave he heard the splash of the incoming water and he realised that what was happening was not a rehearsal. For a moment, he hesitated, then he saw what he had to do.

Where does Curly go from there? TC

———

Once when hove-to in heavy weather and pitching hard I had water siphoned up the exhaust pipe into the engine and another time I sank a launch by a similar oversight. I think the trouble here lies in those cockpit drains which should have been crossed to prevent siphoning. I'm not sure what happened but it sounds like some such nonsense. JDS

———

As Des suggests, in all probability the problem is the cockpit drains. If their cocks are closed the difficulty may resolve itself.

What, however, should be done with Mario and his demands? *Mayday?* Not yet, I hope. The correct message in a situation like this would be to send out a *sécurité* or a *pan* call, and then request that the passing vessel stands by until Curly has either found his problem, or is reduced to genuine distress. TC

Light displacement, lee shore

'How's it going?' Sam peered from the shelter of the companionway at Lilian. Her familiar face was dimly illuminated by the compass light as she took a good look around the horizon.

'As you see, it's about the same as it has been,' retorted Lilian unhappily, 'except that the breeze is up quite noticeably and it seems to have finally decided to rain.'

'No chance of any star sights again, then,' said Sam. He was beginning to get worried. They hadn't seen the sky since they'd shot out of the south end of the Chenal du Four on the corner of France three days ago. Ever since then the *Gallic Galloper*, their brand new, lightweight French-built fast cruiser had been positively flying down towards Spain with a following wind. For a while Sam couldn't believe his luck; the last time he and Lilian had cruised the North Spanish coast had been five years previously in their 24ft Folkboat, and they'd beaten all the way down and then all the way home again. Life in the 28ft *Galloper* had seemed positively charming by comparison as she ran her easy 6 knots before the grey rolling seas with the little autopilot doing all their work for them and the Decca giving tham a regular fix to check against Sam's Estimated Positions. The morning before, however, the Decca had 'gone out', as Sam had predicted it would, because the *Gallic Galloper* had entered the large mid-Biscay gap in the signals.

By now, the boat should have been within range of the Spanish coast coverage, but Sam had no approximate position to give the machine in order to put it back in the picture. He had considered this possibility and so had brought along his old sextant and tables so as to overcome the problem. What he had not bargained for was 48 hours of total overcast, so now, with landfall looming ever closer and a heavy breeze building up, he found himself in a dilemma.

'Fix or not, it's time for the shipping forecast,' said Lilian in her matter-of-fact tone. She went below to tune in the radio and soon the area forecast thundered out its grim prophecy: 'Biscay,

Finisterre. Northerly 7 to severe gale 9, increasing gale 8 to storm 10. Rain, then showers. Poor, becoming moderate.'

Sam made no comment; instead he knocked up a bacon sandwich and was grateful that he'd stowed the mainsail the previous evening. Lilian went on deck and rolled in some more of the furling genoa, then she came below and tapped the barometer. It had been steady at 1013 for 12 hours; now it dipped, but only a point or so. Fortified by his breakfast, Sam consulted the chart and considered his estimated position with all its ghastly implications. At one end of the possibilities he could be 70 or 80 miles offshore, while at the worst, he was within 25 miles of the ironbound north coast of Spain.

For a few mad moments he looked at the possibilities offered by the available ports of refuge, but two problems bulked big in his mind: he didn't know where he was, and before he had identified his landfall in the bad visibility, he could well be smashed up on the rocks. He was not sanguine about the ability of his new yacht to beat off a dead lee shore in force 10.

Better run the motor for a couple of hours, Lilian,' he suggested. 'At least we've plenty of fuel and we don't want flat batteries to add to our joys.' The 20hp diesel started willingly and Sam kitted up and went out on deck to roll in some more genoa.

Out there, in the light of the new day, the wind hit him like a hammer. It had blasted up some more in the past hour and now that they were visible, the seas were impressive. Away on his port beam he saw one begin to break. Sam looked at his storm-jib-sized rolled genoa and smiled wryly. He wished that he had spent his money on an inner forestay and a proper storm jib instead of his now useless electronic navigator, because he had suddenly realised with shocking clarity that he and Lilian were in big trouble.

Dead to leeward was a rocky coast, possibly now less than 25 miles distant. *Gallic Galloper* had no trisail and only the two mainsail reefs supplied by an optimistic manufacturer. Lilian came up on deck wearing her oilskins with her harness and life-jacket jammed on over all.

'I often wondered if we'd regret selling *Folk Melody*,' she said quietly, 'but I never thought it'd be as soon as this.'

The gale howled up another notch and as if to jog Sam into action, a wave slopped into the cockpit. He racked his brains as he considered his options. It didn't seem to him that he had very many.

Sam and Lilian and *Gallic Galloper* are clearly on a set of squeezed isobars between two stable weather systems which means they have small hope of the blow abating significantly for at least 24 hours. How desperate is their situation, and what possible survival tactics are open to them?   TC

––––––

The last thing that Sam and Lilian should do is close the coast in poor visibility and a rising storm. There are two ways by which they might avoid doing so.

The first is to reach out to the west. While the wind is no more than gale force they might achieve this but as it strengthens they will almost certainly have to stow the headsail and they will then make no better than a very broad reach under bare poles. Whether or not they will weather Cape Finisterre depends on how far west they were heading on the Spanish Coast.

The second and probably better option is to heave to under engine. With the big 20hp diesel and plenty of fuel in reserve this is probably their best chance of survival. The tactics would be to turn head to wind, stow all sail, and motor as fast as necessary to remain heading into the sea.

If the weather forecast is right and the visibility improves they probably only need to hold their ground to windward until dusk, when the powerful lights on the Spanish coast should become visible and allow them to line up the Decca and run for shelter. They certainly don't want to remain at sea for longer than is necessary, with only two of them on board their endurance is going to be limited by physical exaustion as much as by any other factor.   BA

––––––

The only suggestion I would add to what Bill recommends is that, if the wind strength remains within the bounds of reason, it is at least

23

possible that the boat will make some progress to windward under engine *AND REEFED MAINSAIL*. If the halyard, reefing pennant, sheet and kicker were set up as hard as possible in order to flatten the sail, it would, if set up almost amidships on the traveller, supply a certain amount of forward drive. It will also steady the boat and help the propeller to grip the water.

This will only work, however, if great care is taken with the steering of the boat. If she is allowed to fall far enough from the wind for the sail to fill completely, she will heel excessively and progress will cease.

Had the boat been equipped with a third reef, or even a trisail, then this technique of motor-sailing gently to windward would certainly have supplied a boat-saving storm survival tactic.   TC

The Bull in the fog

'That'll do nicely,' Joe nodded in satisfaction as he circled his seven-star fix on the chart and entered it in the log. Then he called up to his mate and sole companion. 'Forty-five miles to Cabo Toro, then another three round the corner to Puerto Placido. It's paella and vino collapso for us tonight, boy.'

At the tiller, Andrew watched as the sun's rim broke the horizon dead ahead. He aimed the boat straight for it and waited until it was half a diameter clear. 'Sun bears 077 degrees compass!' he called down to his skipper. It was the usual morning routine, weather permitting.

'Very good.' A couple of minutes went by. 'That's 5 degrees west deviation on this heading. No change.'

Joe ran a tight ship when it came to navigation, thought Andrew, not for the first time. He didn't miss a trick. They'd been at sea the best part of a month now, all the way from the West Indies, and were looking forward to stopping off in Spain for a last fling before heading for home in Devon.

There wasn't a breath of wind and the proximity of the land mass was calming the sea as the 36ft sloop motored steadily on. Andrew ran through the situation in his mind. They had plenty of fuel, so at 5 knots they should be rounding Cabo Toro at about 1430. Loads of time to choose a berth, find a shower, then hit the bistros.

Joe came on deck at 0630, handed Andrew a mug of tea and peered at the dial of the trailing log, rotating merrily on the quarter as it had been doing for the past month. He opened the front and gave it a squirt of oil.

'According to the log and the last two fixes, the current's more or

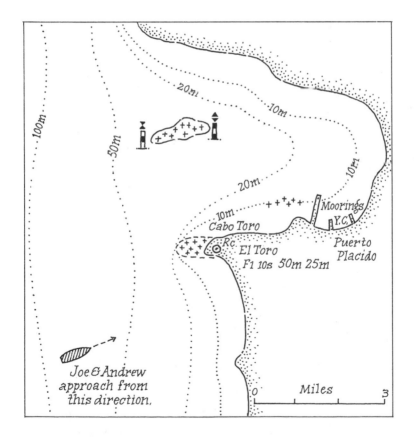

less non-existent,' he said. 'Possibly a quarter knot or so to the south, which you'd expect. It may pick up as we approach the coast.'

And so they motored on through the morning. The shipping built up in density, going in both directions, but by 1100 there was no sign of the high land. Joe watched carefully as the most recent coaster disappeared from view, but she never reached the horizon. Visibility was thickening up.

By noon, they were in dense fog.

'What do you reckon the viz is now?' asked Andrew.

'Pretty academic, I'd say,' replied Joe, observing a seagull as it flew into the murk. 'Fifty yards perhaps.' Joe read the log and went below. A few minutes later Andrew heard the bleeping of Joe's old, but honest RDF set. 'TR . . . TR . . . TR . . .' El Toro light. Then came the sound of Joe skilfully finding the null. Andrew leaned down the hatch just in time to see an EP appearing on the chart comfortingly close to the Position Line from the DF beacon. Joe turned on the echo sounder and checked his depth.

'How does it look?' Andrew was becoming anxious, in spite of his faith in Joe's navigation.

'Well,' mused Joe. 'According to the depth we may, or may not be within two miles of my EP, but that's not so bad after a morning's run.' He spent another ten minutes carefully examining the chart of the approaches to Puerto Placido, tapping his pencil contemplatively as he did so, then he returned the pencil to its rack and came up to the cockpit.

A gentle onshore breeze was picking up, and from somewhere came the drone of a fishing boat's diesels.

'What do you think then, Andrew?' he asked with a grin. 'Shall we go in?'

His mate looked at him humourlessly. 'You're the skipper,' he said. 'You tell me.'   TC

There may well be a way of entering Puerto Placido in 50 yards visibility but I'm not sure that I would trust Joe with the navigation, for two

reasons. First because he takes seven-star sights. Four stars are ample to establish and confirm a position, it might be reasonable to take a fifth just in case the first four leave some ambiguity but to take, reduce and plot seven stars indicates either a lack of confidence or a fixation with sight reduction. Secondly, he is deluding himself if he thinks he is doing something useful by pointing the boat at the rising sun to check the deviation of the compass. It would indeed be useful to check the deviation daily on the heading of the present leg of the voyage but there is no reason why the deviation when steering towards the rising sun should be relevant.

There is no radio beacon or depth contour line which will provide a direct lead into harbour so the plan will have to depend at some stage on a transferred position line.

The key is the line A-B which runs into the bay, passing as far as possible from the two steep-to dangers. The easiest way to get onto this line is to use a transferred position line off El Toro radio beacon.

Alter course to the north and keep going until El Toro is on the required bearing (position w), then run in directly towards it. Note the log reading at the 50m depth contour, continue for half a mile and then alter course 90 degrees to port (position x).

Run the distance by the log to position y and alter course along A−B. The aim is now to run the distance y−z before altering course to east south east to pick up the 10m depth contour line and follow it in a southwesterly direction to find the end of the breakwater. The 20m line will give a clue to the time of arrival at z, but don't rely on it, if you are slightly to starboard of track you will cross the contour line early and if you turn to starboard you may pile into the rocks to the west of the harbour. Between y and z you should be able to confirm your position by a running fix on El Toro radio beacon.

The main hazard is probably going to be fishing boats entering or leaving harbour, intent on sorting out their nets and watching the Decca rather than actually looking where they are going. With only two on board it would make sense to concentrate on keeping a really good lookout rather than have one man with his head buried in the chart table, plotting running fixes. I just hope that Joe will be able to resist the temptation to plot fixes at six minute intervals!   BA

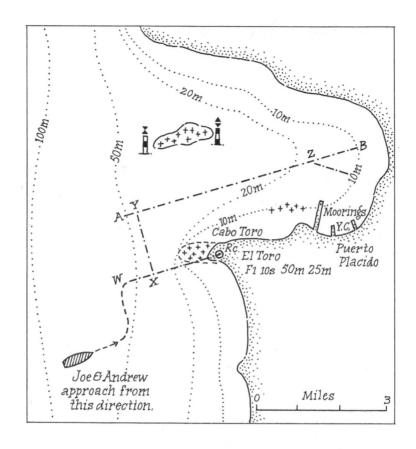

Bill seems to be a trifle hard on Joe by suggesting that he is showing a tendency to over-navigate. I agree entirely that there is no-one worse than the yachtsman who cannot keep himself away from the chart table, particularly when there are more important things to be done. I don't see Joe as one of those.

In practice it takes Joe little longer to reduce and plot seven stars than five if he is using Air Navigation Tables. Stars being what they are, and small boats and their navigators being less than perfect, it is by no means unusual for at least one star out of seven to be a 'discard'. There's also the possibility to consider that Joe might even enjoy it. As any ocean voyager knows, the navigation provides a welcome daily diversion from what some find to be the tedium of watching a great deal of sea for an inordinately long time.

If the sun rises more or less ahead or astern of a yacht on course, nothing could be more natural or seamanlike than to make use of the golden opportunity for a compass check ON THAT HEADING. One can only assume that Joe wouldn't be so naive as to expect this to confirm his complete deviation table! It's interesting to note that the final approach is not very far from 007 degrees, so a check on an adjacent entry in the deviation card would be well worth having for the minimal time it takes to work it out.

I think I'd pin my hopes on Joe. He doesn't seem such a bad lad to me. . . .   TC

Trans-Atlantic daughter

Your daughter Kate is taking a year out between school and university. Her plan is to spend as much time as possible sailing, not, of course, in the family boat but doing her own thing.

She has spent the summer working as a cook/mate at a cruising school. She seems to have learnt a certain amount about sailing and made a great many friends. Among these new-found friends is a group of three girls who are delivering a boat to the West Indies at the end of the season and they have asked Kate to join them.

The boat in question is almost brand new. She is well found and comprehensively equipped. The other three girls and particularly the skipper are undoubtedly competent and experienced, they are all from sailing families and probably learnt to sail before they could ride bicycles. You have few misgivings about the expedition.

You are flattered to be asked to the pre-departure party, the invitation is a tacit acknowledgement that you are still a sailor and a friend, not just a has-been. Half way through the evening you are chatting to the young skipper about her plan for the navigation. It transpires that while the boat is in most respects well equipped the owner is something of a traditionalist and will have no truck with electronic gadgetry, distance run is measured by a trailing log, depth with a lead and there is, of course, no Decca, Loran or Satnav. The only concession is an excellent radio receiver with a direction finding aerial.

The skipper has never actually used a sextant before and her knowledge of astro-navigation is, to put it mildly, limited. She has been too busy preparing the boat to do any studying but she is confident that she will have no problem making an accurate landfall in Antigua. She does know that the simplest sight to take is a meridian altitude and she reckons that at the worst she will be able to put the boat on the right latitude and run down the westing. She hopes that she will learn how to take morning and afternoon sun sights and perhaps even star sights during the passage.

Kate and the other two members of the crew know and accept that this is the intended method of navigation. Your suggestion that the landfall in the Canaries, the only planned port of call, could be tricky is dismissed on the grounds that they will have good radio fixes off the Spanish and Portuguese coasts and Mount Tiede in Tenerife is visible from 60 miles, well within the limits of accuracy of the DR after a relatively short passage of a few hundred miles.

Are you still happy about this expedition? They don't sail until the day after tomorrow so you would have time to buy them a Satnav as a farewell present. You know that Kate respects your judgement and if you asked her to pull out of the crew then she would almost certainly do so.

What are you going to do?   BA

It seems that the young skipper has fallen into the trap much beloved of her age group in each succeeding generation. She has an unshakeable belief in her own immortality.

As far as the Atlantic Crossing from Tenerife to Antigua is concerned, she is proposing to operate on the ancient and well-tried principle of the five

'L's, viz. 'Latitude, Lead, Log, Lookout and trust in the Lord'. In those swashbuckling times before the general availability of longitude this system supplied a workable method of finding an oceanic destination. So long as you knew whether you were east or west of the place to start with you had merely to place your ship on the correct latitude and then run it down until you arrived.

'All very well,' you may think. 'No problem.' But hang on. The mariners of old who operated this principle were a sight more aware of their environment than we are, and they usually were in less of a hurry. When Bjarni Herjolfsson used the system in the tenth century to find Cape Farewell in Greenland, he and his men had senses honed to a sharpness we can never comprehend. Viking seamen regularly traversed the North Atlantic without compass, chart, longitude or any accurate system for measuring distance run. Try that for a few generations and you'll find you can sense the proximity of land using feelers the rest of us have forgotten we have. Take Columbus and his boys: they'd spent a life-time at sea, and there were plenty of them aboard the Santa Maria. There was no shortage of frightened lookouts to search the horizon for breakers. And so on. Those men, when they were closing their destination, would heave to at night so as not to run down the reefs in the dark, and if there was anything at all to see, either by direct vision or by implication from other signs, they would pick it up.

What about Kate and Co? A bunch of students, pampered by sailing in modern yachts. Their lead-line won't be the deep sea lead used by mariners in the seventeenth century. ('We found 50 fathoms on a fine sandy bottom.') It will be one of those small, clean little items that might have been issued by Santa Claus. Not a lot of use for picking up soundings out of the deeps. The girls will be under pressure from their peers to make a fast passage. The nonsense of cruising sailors with different types of boat boasting to one another of their voyage times has become common practice in recent years, so the temptation to drive on through the night will become strong as Antigua is approached. Their log, rather than being a help on a trip like this is likely to lead them into a false sense of security. The essence of navigation is always to be checking one source of information against another. If the log is their only means of finding 'longitude' they are in

31

trouble. Even in the unlikely event of it being accurate to within one per cent, the current is an unknown factor with no astro position against which to compare the DR. They could easily be 250 miles out by the time they reach the other side. If they don't heave to at night and the air is full of Sahara dust, as it sometimes is in those parts, and the skipper is 30 miles or so out in her totally unpractised sextant work, then Kate could end up feeding the fish on the reefs to windward of Barbuda.

And what about finding Tenerife? Anyone who has sailed to the Canaries knows full well that it is the exception rather than the rule for Tiede to be visible before the cliffs or the lights at the north end of the island come into view. Visibility is just not that good down there. The Arctic, now, that would be different, but kids will keep searching for the bubble pleasure of sun worship. . . .

The young lady thinks her DR will be fair after 'a few hundred miles'. I wish her luck.

You'll notice that so far, we've made no mention of the RDF set. This may prove useful, but to cite the ancient chestnut: 'What if it goes on the blink?' There are a hundred reasons for engine failure, some of which may be beyond the capacity of a trained engineer to fix on board. My experience of the approach of many first class young lady sailors to engines is summed up by a 24-year-old sailing instructress overheard briefing her crew. She gave them a thorough description of all the rig, sails, gear, safety equipment, galley etc, then added as an afterthought, 'Oh yes. And the engine's in there. It's red.' She, and hundreds like her have not the faintest idea of even how to bleed a diesel, let alone clear the commutator on a defunct starter motor. Simple tasks you think. Yes, but can these girls keep the engine running come what may so as to feed the batteries without which the RDF set is just so much scrap iron?

If the DF were a luxury, this wouldn't be critical, but since it is of prime importance and no electrical device should ever be relied upon exclusively in a small vessel offshore, it should be discounted completely when considering Kate's immediate future.

There have been several irresponsible young women in recent years who have sailed off into the blue with no knowledge of astro navigation, and have 'taught themselves as they went'. Irresponsible, not because they did it, but because they made capital out of bragging to the world's press that they had done it. If they'd gone wrong, and many people do, they'd have killed themselves or, even worse, become a burden on the search and rescue services who have better things to do. These were exceptionally able people and they were lucky. To publicise their lack of knowledge and the fact that, by the mercy of Allah, they got away with their folly, is to encourage others like Kate's skipper to do likewise. These people are culpable, and Kate may end up the victim of their vanity.

In all probability, the skipper will work it out, at least as far as latitude by Meridian Passage of the sun is concerned, but there is a recently recorded instance of a sane and courageous yachtsman who tried to do just this and ended up in Brazil instead of the Caribbean. He had applied declination the wrong way, and there was no-one aboard to put him right.

No, as things stand, I'm afraid Kate shouldn't go. If I were her, I'd be furious with my so-called skipper who used all her time to work up a simple boat and neglected to spend the few days, which for an intelligent young girl, is all it would have taken, to learn the rudiments of celestial navigation.

Kate's only hope is to come down to my study with a bag of ice on her head and spend the next 24 hours coming to grips with Declination, LHA, and the Sight Reduction Tables for Air Navigat on. As an alternative to the abridged full story, I might even consider teaching her the principles and limitations of 'longitude by equal angles' as a workable short cut when running down a latitude in the tropics. Then we'll take out the old brass sextant and practise on the hill ridge five miles away across the Dale. If she can thoroughly convince me, then I'll give her the green light.

It's not impossible for someone her age, used to learning, but it's a tall order.

I've every faith in Kate's common sense so if she manages the figures and the sextant, I'll buy her a Satnav to check her sights against and vice versa with one per cent of my last Saturday's winnings on the races. But if she hasn't got a grip of the basics I'll save my money and advise her to stay at home, because a Satnav is subject to the same potential difficulties as the RDF. Besides, I didn't put the satellites up there and I don't personally know the individual who did. They might break down.   TC

Tom's sense of adventure is no doubt tempered with fears of what could go wrong, all from personal experience, no doubt. There have been many examples of young men and women setting out to 'discover themselves'. Most survive to tell the tale, but a parent has a duty to point out the dangers, even if the advice is usually ignored. My advice would be to give Kate a plastic sextant, copies of the Admiralty Nautical Almanac, the Air Navigation Tables and a good book on celestial navigation, preferably Mary Blewitt's *Astro Navigation for Yachtsmen*. Then two of them can practice taking sights and even when they reach the Canaries at least one of them should have achieved some degree of proficiency. At all costs avoid trying to persuade them to rush into fitting a Satnav, a rushed installation could be positively dangerous, particularly if none of the crew know how to use the thing.   BA

Fog

The fairway buoy was abeam as the fog rolled in.

James said a mental 'Thank you' to his guardian angel. An hour ago 50 yards visibility would have made for a hit or miss landfall but now it was no more than inconvenient. The river was well buoyed all the way to the marina. The flood stream ran true along the line of the channel so it should be simple to lay off the courses from buoy to buoy along the starboard side of the channel. If he kept a close eye on the echo sounder it would give ample warning if he was wandering over the shallows and the width of the buoyed fairway was no more than 100 yards so he should pick up a port hand buoy if he got off track to port.

James asked Dick to hoist the radar reflector and then to keep a lookout from the foredeck. He eased the throttle back slightly to settle the speed at exactly four knots. Then he turned over the steering to Elizabeth and went below to the chart table.

The first three starboard hand buoys appeared exactly on schedule. Elizabeth was obviously doing a good job on the helm and any element of tension which James had felt had gone, he was totally relaxed.

'Tell Dick that Long Reach buoy should be visible in 30 seconds,' he called to Elizabeth and heard her relay the message to the foredeck.

Two minutes later there was no sign of the buoy. The echo sounder showed that they were still in the channel, or at least very close to it. In this reach there were gently shelving mud banks on both sides, so they would have to be quite a long way off track before the depth altered much.

James left the chart table and climbed into the cockpit. 'Knock her out of gear would you' he said to Elizabeth. The revs died and the speed dropped. The fog was, if anything, slightly thicker, a featureless grey blanket on all sides. He was about to go below when the blast of the fog horn sounded astern of them.

Nobody said a word but the same thoughts were going through the minds of all of them. The only ships which used the river were the ferries, 350ft long, 80 ft wide. The ferry berth was a mile up river from the marina and the ferries were difficult enough to keep clear of in good visibility. The fog horn sounded again, noticeably louder this time. They couldn't just wait where they were, they had to do something. But what?   BA

James' mistake has been to try to buoy-hop in a situation where he had an alternative. We are not given much detail about this river, but we have enough information to know that at the time of the foghorn, visibility is probably less than 50 yards. We are also told by inference that the buoys are not right at the edge of the water navigable by small vessels. The danger to which James and Co have laid themselves open is that they may miss one buoy for any number of sound reasons. They will then be on their way to becoming lost as they now are, though not, as we shall see, beyond redemption.

A preferable tactic when the circumstances offer it, as they do in this case, is to run up the river along a depth contour ideally on the starboard side, but certainly outside the channel. This is not in any way dangerous, especially with a flooding tide to float the boat off the mud in the event of a mishap. Had James opted to do this he would, in all probability, have seen the occasional buoy go by on his port side, offering him a fix of his position. If the marina were on this starboard side of the river, he would have no more to do than stay on his contour until he arrived at the outer berths. If, however, the marina is on the port side, he might have done better to have chosen to keep himself out of the channel on that side of the river instead. So long as he was clear of the shipping channel it would be of no great importance which side he chose, though his starboard would be better, all things being equal.

The way to run a contour is for James to decide what depth he wants to see on his echo sounder and then run into shoaling water on a course 20 degrees inshore of the compass 'heading' of the contour. When the chosen depth is crossed, he then turns 40 degrees offshore so as to rapidly deepen the water once more. Then he turns in again, and so on, unless of course he can find the exact heading to keep him plumb down the line. In other words, he is steering on compass and echo sounder only. His log will give him an idea of when his destination should be due to appear, and the combined eyes of the crew should be on the lookout for any useful fixed objects looming up to confirm their current position.

James, unfortunately, didn't do this.

At the time that he hears the foghorn he is, in all probability, outside the channel to starboard. This is because with something approaching 50 yards visibility, had he missed Long Reach by passing to port of it he could well have been lucky enough to see a port-hand buoy.

This conclusion is not certain; it is merely the balance of probabilities.

What he must therefore do is to turn to starboard, whichever side of the channel he is actually on, or even if he is, in fact, in the middle. He then motors slowly at 90 degrees to the channel, heading for the starboard bank, and ever so gently, runs his yacht up the mud where she is safe from being run down.

He'll know when the big ship goes by because she will take half the river with her and, for a short time, James, Dick and Elizabeth may find themselves on their beam ends.

When the water returns, James can use full astern to pull himself off, helped by the flooding tide. At least he now knows on which side of the river he is and can begin running a suitable contour to his destination if it is on that side. If it should be on the other side, he must cross the channel and work up the opposite bank instead.

He'll just have to hope that he hasn't already blundered past the place in the fog, but if he has, he'll know it when he comes abeam of the ferry terminal, which he will certainly be able to hear, even if he doesn't see it. Then he must find his contour from this known position, and work back to that marina and a nice, relaxing shower.   TC

———

I agree. Head at right angles to the line of the channel and make for shallow water. Better to err on the shallow side and run aground rather than risk being run down by the ferry. A grounding on a rising tide is no problem. Being clobbered by a ship is.   BA

Short handed

George cursed Max Wentworth. It was a somewhat empty gesture, as Max was 300 miles away, recovering from a bout of 'flu and George was 70 miles southwest of Ushant, on passage towards Spain.

The leg down Channel from Chichester had been hard going, dead to windward every inch of the way and with only three of them on board they were all getting tired. Max would have been the fourth member of the crew, if he had not been stricken by the 'flu bug, which would have made two in each watch and much easier sailing.

Aida, the Contessa 32 which they were sailing, had no self-steering gear and although she would take herself to windward with the headsail sheeted hard and the main eased slightly, George had decided that they should always have two men on watch. This meant that they had been working six hours on, three hours off for over two days and the strain was beginning to tell.

'I've had about as much of this as I can take,' said Rob. 'I reckon we've either got to change the watch system or run off into port for a day's rest.'

'And I quite agree,' John chipped in. 'We'd be fine with one on watch, then we could do two hours on, four off. I'm not keen on heading for a French port and throwing away ground that we've won to windward but I don't think I can keep going much longer with this long watch short sleep routine!'

George knew exactly how his two crewmen felt. He was tired himself and there was a strong temptation to go along with their suggestion. The problem was that neither of them were very experienced sailors and if they did change the watchkeeping roster for an easier routine he knew that he probably wouldn't be able to sleep with either of them on watch on their own, particularly at night.

Their discussion was interrupted by the 1355 shipping forecast. It promised no change from the present southwesterly force 5 and moderate visibility with occasional rain.

George knew that they couldn't just continue with their punishing watch-keeping routine. They had at least another two and a half days at sea and if he persisted with the present system he would probably have a mutiny on his hands.

What should he do?   BA

As I have found to my cost fatigue can lead to dangerous errors, a greater risk than George doing a one-man watch. He should revise the watch system to give two six-hour daylight watches, he taking a lone one, and three-hour night watches either overlapping as before or two and one.

High time the skipper learned to trust his crew to call him if in doubt! JDS

————

Basically I agree with the answer Des has given but I think the following would be helpful.

An equally good way of solving the fatigue problem would be a hybrid watch system, with two people on watch by night but only one by day, something along the following lines:

Time.	On Watch	Off Watch
0000–0300	A + B	C
0300–0600	C + A	B
0600–0900	C	A + B
0900–1200	B	C + A
1200–1500	A	B + C
1500–1800	C	A + B
1800–2100	B	C + A
2100–2359	A + B	C

Everyone gets at least two unbroken six-hour periods of rest in 24 hours. You may have to adjust the times of the breaks between watches to fit in with dawn and dusk and have a system of 'first to be called if an extra man is needed' so that everybody has one long rest guaranteed, although their other long rest period may be disturbed if a sail change is needed. BA

Physician heal thyself

Tom was a neophyte Yachtmaster Instructor. It was his first season and he was keen and inventive. He was also perfectly naive about the level of competence, experience and plain commonsense to expect from some of his students, even at Coastal Skipper level.

He had learned all about structuring his week's work so as to leave time to grab any opportunity that offered itself to cover a practical item from the comprehensive syllabus that looked as though it might be missed by the conventional passagemaking course format: he'd also gleaned a host of useful tips from his own instructor about how to engineer teaching situations. By Friday morning, this particular course had dealt with every major topic in the book, but one. Two of his students were shaping up wonderfully at boathandling under power, a third was managing not to splinter the dock as he came alongside, but the fourth seemed as though he would be best advised to take up golf. It was a typical week, but so far, they had not picked up a single mooring under sail.

Now, bowling home up the Solent before a force 4 westerly with 3 knots of tide behind them, it seemed that the opportunity was not going to be there at all. Cowes Week was approaching and all the 'safe' buoys in the home river would be taken, and so Tom decided to use his training and initiative. He sailed over to the Island shore to the area off Newtown Creek, where it is possible to anchor in the open water, directed his crew to prepare the kedge, then brought his 32ft yacht to the wind and tide and anchored immaculately.

When the kedge was well and truly dug in, he buoyed the end of the warp, which was of the type that sinks, and announced that this was now to be designated a mooring. Each of his crew were to have the opportunity to pick it up and to leave it under sail only.

It seemed a good idea at the time and everything went smoothly for skipper one and two. Skipper number three's effort should have shown Tom the red light but it was the golfer who really taught his leader a thing or two. This honest fellow did not approach the buoy across the tide, spilling wind on a close reach, as the others had done. He was suffering from what is known in the trade as a 'dynamic environmental awareness problem', in other words, he didn't have a clue what was happening. He roared down-tide at the dancing anchor buoy and stuffed his helm down at the last minute in order to luff. The boat luffed all right, but she carried her way clear across the anchor warp, lurching to a halt as the rope, guided inexorably by the fin keel and detached rudder, took a snaking turn around the propeller, or its 'P' bracket, or both. The tide did the rest and within a matter of seconds, our hero found himself moored by the propeller in a 3 knot tide, heading dead downwind with both sails drawing beautifully, and the buoy somewhere out of sight beneath the yacht.

The kedge, firmly set by the previous manoeuvres, held like a concrete block and there, as they say, things came to rest.

Here was an item that didn't appear on the syllabus and with which Tom had never before had to contend. He hadn't time to wait for slack water, and one sample pull from the dinghy at the weight of the kedge warp showed him that his vaunted initiative was about to be searchingly examined.

'Pity the management didn't supply an outboard for the tender,' he thought ruefully, as he eyed the pitiful, toy-town paddles.

Did he make it back to Cowes in time for lunch? If so, how?   TC

Of course he made it back in time for lunch. He whipped out the bolt croppers, snipped the kedge warp, bought the secrecy of the crew with promises of pints of beer and told the chief instructor a very plausible story about the motor cruiser which had sliced through the kedge warp.

On second thoughts, perhaps that would be rather too slick a solution for our tyro instructor.

The first priority must be to get the sails off her to reduce the weight on the warp or the problem is going to be compounded by a bent shaft.

The dinghy is going to be useless for taking anything — the bower anchor or a tripping line — up tide. Progress will simply not be possible with only one pair of short paddles. The dinghy should, however, be useful as a working platform, first to pass a line under the warp to pull it clear of the water and then to rolling-hitch a relieving line to it about 15ft astern of the yacht.

The relieving line can then be used to start heaving in on the kedge warp, leading it to a sheet winch to achieve the very considerable power

that will be needed. As soon as enough slack (it will need a little over two boats' lengths) has been recovered the kedge warp can be taken forward and in through the stem-head roller and the yacht can then be swung to lie normally to the kedge.

As soon as the weight is off the bitter end of the kedge warp the buoy will probably come bobbing to the surface.

If it doesn't it will be necessary to weigh anchor, sail out into clear water, heave to and do some exploring with a boat hook from the dinghy to retrieve the buoy.

The recovery operation is going to involve much heaving, hauling, sweating and searching for appropriate lengths of spare line. It might well be a late lunch at Cowes. BA

———

What a good idea about the bolt croppers! For those with less moral fibre, however, Bill's second solution is surely a winner. TC

A valuable short cut

It was a quiet evening when they locked out of the harbour and headed for sea, so quiet in fact that the temptation to take a five-mile short cut over the shallows couldn't be resisted. With the many beacon towers and marks available it was just a matter of careful chart reading. Then the breeze failed and the engine stopped simultaneously and they had to kedge. It took a couple of hours to get the machinery back in business but by then dusk was falling and so was a thin drizzle which reduced visibility to a couple of cables. Soon it would be quite dark and none of the beacons were lighted. Whether they stood on or turned back it was suddenly vital to know the rate and direction of the tidal stream.

The available information was sketchy, the general set was to the north west at 1–2 knots but was this also true for the inshore shallows? They could bet some idea of tidal set from the flow of water past the anchored yacht but would this help them further on? More to the point there was a freshening breeze from ahead which would alter the lie of the boat. Plainly they couldn't lie there until morning but if they pressed on it was vital to know the set of the tide so that a safe heading could be plotted through the rocks and reefs which lay ahead.

Since they had to beat the gathering darkness they got under way at once while they could still see the beacons close ahead. The navigator gave the helmsman a heading to steer, 'Keep her as straight as you possibly can for the next ten minutes or so then I'll give you another course,' he said. What plan had he in mind?   JDS

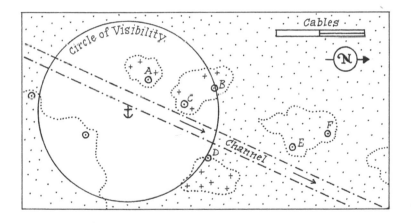

Before leaving, regardless of the lie of the boat the navigator should have been able to assess the rate and set of the tidal stream quite accurately by looking at his own anchor cable. He should also have plotted his position on anchoring before the visibility closed in with a three point fix so he has a good departure point. This will give him enough information to go searching for his next objective, beacon D, just out of sight. Initially it

won't be easy for him to fix his position but as soon as beacon B resolves itself a transit of C and B and a bearing on A will give him a fair idea of the effect of the stream when he compares course steered with his track. Beacon D will be in sight and he will by now have given the helmsman an updated course to steer. As he comes abeam of D he will be able to pass the beacon close enough again to check the rate and set on the base of the beacon and shortly after he will again have an excellent opportunity to obtain an accurate position and once more compare course steered with track. A transit of E and F crossed with a bearing of B, still just within his circle of visibility will be enough to confirm his calculations and lay off a course with confidence to take him clear of the shallows.   *AB*

Yes. The beacons ahead and to port C–B give a useful transit which crossed by beacon A a reliable fix. If this puts him square in the channel he can steer xxx mag until A–C are in transit and crossed by a bearing on D, any tidal set will then be apparent and can be corrected in a revised heading. Or, if the first position put him to the east of the channel he might steer straight for beacon D, a course roughly parallel to the channel. The heading needed to keep D on the bow would be the heading needed for the channel.   JDS

On the beach

It was a lovely day by anyone's standards and the single-handed yachtsman saw no possibility of trouble from the weather as he coasted along gently in the light onshore breeze that warm morning. There was only one thing troubling him, the urgent phone call he should have made to his office and lacking VHF radio and a link call it was becoming vital that he got to a phone box. The coast was innocent looking with its long stretch of beach and inland he could see a small village among the trees. Why not anchor for half an hour while he nipped ashore in the dinghy?

The holding ground he suspected was not of the best, gravelly stuff, but the breeze was so light that the yacht barely even straightened out her anchor warp. With only a backwards glance he strode off inland and within a short while he was in a phone box. Then the trouble began, the person he wished to speak with was out but due back in a few minutes. The yachtsman, containing his impatience, repaired to a teashop for ten minutes then phoned again; still no success. It was a full hour before he reached his colleague on the phone and by then he was uneasily aware that the trees were tossing lazily in a strengthening onshore breeze, he hastened back to the beach. To his horror he found that his yacht was ashore, beam on against a steep-to beach and grinding as she rolled and crashed in the rising sea. It was not a terminal situation, not yet, the tide was making and would be for the next couple of hours so he must act quickly.

With huge relief he saw a fishing boat making for the scene. There was no point in pretending that this was not a salvage matter so he surrendered gladly to the fishermen's expertise. They heaved a line ashore which he made fast to the bows of the yacht, but despite repeated attempts to haul her off the yacht remained pinned against the steep curve of the beach. He considered running back to the phone and trying to raise more help but time was against him,

what might the weather be doing by the next high water? If only they could haul her bows seawards she would lift on the waves and perhaps then she could be towed off, but how?   JDS

———————

Oh Dear! Our hero has, as my grandfather used to say, brought his pigs to an unfortunate market.

Clearly, the fishing boat just does not have that edge of power that it will take to do the business, but the yachtsman is probably quite right to persevere with the help available and put all possible effort into getting off on this tide rather than running for the phone. There is still plenty that can be done, bearing in mind that the tide has two hours to rise.

Here are the most likely courses of action which, separately or together, should save the day. If the others fail, the final solution is almost certain to produce a result:

(i) The yacht's own anchor is still out there somewhere. Presumably she was originally anchored in somewhat deeper water than she now finds herself, so the scope of the cable must exceed the minimum normally required for a 'bite on the bottom'. Even if the hook were foolishly not dug in when it was laid, it may respond to the treatment now. The first thing to do then, is to heave in on the anchor rode. If the anchor sets itself in spite of the poor ground, then the spring in the nylon warp as the boat pounds may prove sufficient to help the fishing boat bring the yacht's head round. Obviously, care must be taken to communicate with the rescuing vessel lest she foul her propeller on the newly tightened anchor rode.

(ii) Why not start the yacht's engine as well? If the tiller is put hard towards the beach and the yacht is motored full ahead, the extra life this gives her as she bounces may enable the fishing craft to do her work.

(iii) Hoisting sail is unlikely to be of assistance on a lee shore, since the sails will tend to drive the boat up the beach. This is because very little forward drive is delivered from a sail to a boat until she begins to move. However, this is a time for desperate measures and the situation is far from the usual one when an unassisted yacht is stranded on a lee shore. We have

a powerful tug pulling the boat's bows to seaward, the very thing the sails cannot do at the moment. What the sails will do, is to heel the boat over and, assuming she is a fin keeler, reduce her draft. As a last ditch, this may be worth trying, but on no account should sail be hoisted forward of the mast, as this will tend to push the bows 'down' and hold the yacht's head onto the beach.

(iv) The fishing boat is not succeeding in her efforts because she is, in effect, losing 'traction', just like a car trying to tow another vehicle out of a muddy field. If a winch whose wire is made fast to a stout gate-post can be put on the front of the towing car, the combined effect of the pull of the winch and the drive of the car's own wheels will often succeed.

(v) In a case where a tug just cannot pull a stranded boat off a lee shore, it is of enormous benefit to stream out the tow warp to the largest possible length, then lay of the tug's bower anchor well to seaward. The tug can then fall back laying cable as she does so until the maximum possible scope has been achieved. Even if the holding ground is indifferent, the massive scope will go a long way to compensate for it.

All that now remains is for the fishing boat to lead the anchor cable to her trawl or pot winch if she has no windlass, and to heave away while motoring full ahead. The yacht can assist by any or all of the means described above, and if that lot doesn't succeed in hauling her off, then it's time to go back to the telephone box and call for a Dutch salvage tug!   TC

———

Tom Cunliffe contributes different but valuable tips for dealing with the problem of a boat on the beach. But watch that temperature gauge if using the engine. There'll be a lot of sand or mud churned up so close to the shore, but perhaps that's the least of their worries now. Another solution is this.

The use of a powerful lever may work and what better lever than the yacht's mast? It is a trick which has been used with success in such desperate circumstances although there is always a risk that the mast might be pulled out of the boat but since she may become a total loss if left there it is a worthwhile gamble. The fishing boat crew would need to retain their tow rope to the bows but take a second line to a couple of the halyards and with the tow rope slack endeavour to pull on the masthead at a slight angle. Once the yacht had been slewed round to face seawards the tow would have to be transferred to her bows. Not an easy operation and calling for expert boat handling.   JDS

Swinging room

Yacht *Betty* came into the anchorage with barely a breath of wind and as her crew didn't intend to stay long they anchored her on a bare scope, just enough to suit the calm and gentle conditions. They had been on passage all night and after a quick meal they got their heads down for a couple of hours rest. Meanwhile, in mid-afternoon *Teal* came in and her crew had a very different plan in mind, they had heard the latest weather forecast and they knew that it was going to blow. There wasn't a great deal of room in the anchorage though and assuming that *Betty* was lying to a normal scope they let go to one side of and ahead of her dropping astern to a generous scope of cable.

Then *Betty*'s crew woke up and looked around. They found that the sky had clouded over and a freshening breeze was getting up, the skipper called up on VHF for a weather forecast and upon hearing what was pending plans were altered and it was decided to remain in the anchorage instead of getting under way. Remembering that they had anchored on a short scope they paid out some more.

While wind and current were opposing the two yachts remained well separated but when the tide turned and both yachts lay head to wind and current *Betty* began to drag. By now though they were very close, *Teal* lying to leeward of *Betty*. 'I need to pay out more scope and you have given me a foul berth,' *Betty*'s skipper shouted to the other owner. 'I can't pay out any more or I'll foul the boat astern of me' *Teal*'s owner shouted back, 'and I'm certainly not going to move for you, I've nowhere else to go, *you'll* have to pick up and shift your anchor further to windward.'

It was a stalemate. *Betty*'s owner said that they'd been anchored first and therefore they had right of way in the matter. *Teal*'s owner said that he had been properly anchored and *Betty* had not been anchored properly. Which would you vote for?   JDS

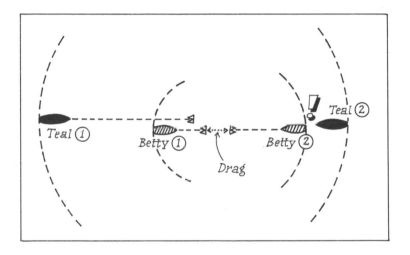

Clearly this dispute isn't going to be resolved in gentlemanly fashion. I'm probably wrong but I would vote for Teal. *I would consider that the first come, first served principle only held good if* Betty *had been properly anchored in the first place.* Teal's *crew arrived and in view of the forecast* Betty's *crew had missed while they were asleep had to make the assumption that they were lying to the appropriate scope. If* Betty's *crew been properly anchored and if she hadn't dragged then the onus would be on* Teal *to move. But in this case as* Betty *is dragging − a situation* Teal *could not have foreseen − it is her responsibility to weigh and relay her anchor in a position to give her enough scope to hold.*

Even if Teal *had agreed to move to allow* Betty *room to lay more scope, there is still doubt as to whether she would be able to lay enough cable to hold without fouling the boat astern. One can only hope that* Teal's *crew will offer to help* Betty *move and re-anchor.* AB

In the ordinary course of events *Betty*'s skipper would have been in the right for a vessel has a right to a clear swinging space and later arrivals who deny her this right have given her a foul berth. However, while *Teal* had been anchored with care and in a seamanlike manner, it might be argued that *Betty* had been anchored negligently and that *Teal*'s owner was not to know this and would assume that *Betty* was already lying to a proper scope. Of course such a fracas should never have been allowed to develop between fellow yachtsmen faced with a common danger. JDS

Counting their chickens . . .

It was just as well that it was almost a flat calm because the roller of the roller headsail was jammed solid leaving them with a whole genoa set and no means of either lowering or reducing it. There was only another three and a half miles to go for the port and the end of the charter holiday and the crew felt relieved, it wasn't a pleasant feeling to know that the boat was no longer capable of being reefed down in the event of the calm being replaced by a freshening breeze – by no means an improbability.

Another small worry was that the engine was ailing and three knots was all that it could give them, moreover they had only three hours of fuel left. The tidal stream had gone foul an hour ago and it was running against them at a knot, too deep to kedge until it went fair again and the only alternative shelter haven was now ten miles astern. The skipper looked at the sky and pursed his lips, a bit of greasy looking cloud was beginning to gather. Still, there was only three and a half miles to go. The rest of the crew had begun discussing the pros and cons of eating aboard when they got in or going out on the town.

The skipper wasn't very experienced but for some reason he felt that such plans were premature, he felt uneasy. Only three and a half miles to go though. Had he good reason for feeling a bit uneasy?   JDS

––––––––

The skipper is quite right to be apprehensive. At sea once can never feel comfortable unless one knows that one can shorten sail.

In fact, though, he doesn't have an isoluble problem – all he has to do is emulate the Ooslum bird, the species which became extinct because its protective manoeuvre was to fly round in circles until it disappeared up its own tail. Unfortunately it never discovered a way of reversing the vanishing act.

Although it may be impossible to rotate the stay round the inside of the sail, as soon as there is a reasonable breeze it should be quite easy to rotate the sail around the outside of the stay. The first move should be to attach a short sheet, four or five metres long, to the clew of the sail and remove the working sheets. We all know what happens to an ensign when we sail round in circles. The genoa should behave in exactly the same way. Sail round in a few circles, pause head to wind and heave on the sheet to neaten down the furl and continue until the area has been reduced by the required amount.

Our hero won't have the insoluble problem which destroyed the Ooslum bird, his vanishing genoa can be made to re-appear simply by reversing the direction of rotation.   BA

––––––––

Bill Anderson is so keen to pass on his excellent tips for dealing with a jammed roller headsail that he seems to have missed my trap concerning the steadily increasing tidal rate, but no matter! The harbour is three and a half miles ahead and at three knots they have nine miles of motoring left, but the foul tide has already attained a rate of one knot by the end of the first hour. Since tidal rate obeys the same rule as tidal rise and fall the rate will increase towards the middle of the six hour (roughly) period and tail off again towards the end before going slack and then turning. Remembering the old rule-of-thumb that a tide runs at one third of its maximum rate during the first and sixth hours then two thirds during the second and fifth hours, full rate during the third and fourth hours, since it had already attained one knot by the end of the first hour their speed of three knots means that they will only make one knot over the ground in the next hour and none at all once the rate of current reaches its full three knots. On the other hand to turn and go back ten miles with that rate of tide under them means they'll complete the distance in a couple of hours.   JDS

Not a good start to the day

The boat was long of keel, heavy displacement and until they could find an engineer to help, temporarily engineless, but they found a cozy anchorage at the top of the creek and there passed a peaceful night. Came the morning though they found that the wind was now blowing slap into the creek and that to leeward there ran a row of evil-looking rotting piles. Just for good measure another boat now lay blocking their exit from the creek, well not blocking it entirely.

They had a choice. They would have to beat out of course, but it was a choice of breaking out anchor on the starboard tack and thereafter tacking again very smartly before they ran out of water and then weathering the stranger who blocked the channel or of breaking out on port tack. This, however, would mean sailing over the shallow mud flats with perhaps only a foot of water under their keel, tacking as soon as they could before they ran into even shallower water. 'We'll break out on starboard' the skipper decided, 'we'll wait until there's a bit of ebb running though so that we can be sure of clearing that other boat on the next tack!

Of course it didn't work out that way, instead of breaking out on starboard tack she snubbed on her anchor, cast round on to port tack and *then* it broke out. Off they went over the shallows at a spanking pace. 'She won't steer!' yelled the helmsman,' she feels dead, we must have fouled something.' The boat wouldn't tack. They paid off again and lumbered ahead, rapidly making for still shallower water. . . .

Well they got out of that one and the open sea lay ahead. The skipper was on the helm. 'Give me a course down this channel' he told the crew in general. Down below someone was reading the pilot book. 'It says here that the deep water channel lies 210 degrees skipper', he said. The skipper put 210 degrees on the steering compass and all was peace aboard.

How did they get out of that tacking situation and was all really destined to remain peace aboard?   JDS

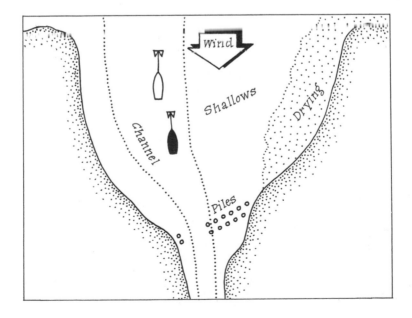

(i) The Tacking Problem

The boat is experiencing difficulty in tacking for one of two reasons. Either she is sailing through very soft mud, or she is still drudging her anchor behind her. In either case, there is only one thing to do. She dare not risk bearing away in order to 'wear round' in case she goes solidly aground on the shallows when she is dead before the wind.

She needs to get onto the other tack, and fast, but she cannot gather enough way to 'stay'. She has an anchor already trailing from her bow on a short scope, or at least hanging from the stemhead roller awaiting proper stowage. Her best chance of putting her head through the wind lies in letting the anchor run for a couple of boats' lengths until it has a substantial scope, then to snub off the cable and, as soon as the crew see that the anchor is biting to put the helm down to leeward as hard as possible. As the yacht begins to come towards the wind the anchor will assist the process by snubbing her head right round. Her headsail should be left aback to make sure of the manoeuvre.

Once on the desired starboard tack she will find herself across and partially upward from the anchor, so she must sail back to it, as slowly as possible, *her crew gathering cable as she does so. With the wind abaft the beam slowing down is not easy, but the best way in this case is to let fly the headsail sheet and to sheet the main hard amidships, stalling it completely. This won't help the steering, but it will certainly stop the boat going so fast that the foredeck hand loses any fingers he has left.*

As she sails over the anchor for the last time, it can be plucked clear of the bottom without drama and hauled up to the stemhead, where the prudent skipper of an engineless boat will leave it, ready for any further trouble, until he is clear out to sea.

The yacht is now in a fair position to give the other boat a wide berth and to beat out to seaward in an orderly manner.

The only circumstance that would render this tacking operation ineffective would be if the ebb tide were so strong that the yacht was being carried to windward of her anchor cable. The seems an unlikely contingency as both boats were clearly lying solidly to the wind at the outset, but once the boat starts sailing and her keel gets a grip on the moving water, the possibility cannot be discounted. If this is happening, the symptom will be refusal to tack using the instructions above and the only thing for the crew to do is to dig in the anchor, as described, then drag down the mainsail as quickly as possible. The boat can then be pulled back to the anchor gybing round under headsail alone as her crew hauls away. Once on the starboard tack with the anchor weighed and aboard, there should be room to luff and rehoist the main smartly in preparation for the beat down-river.

(ii) The Course to Steer

In the first place, channels in pilot books are generally designated in degrees true from seaward. In this instance, presumably an exception has been made. The course offered by the casual pilot book reader down below must at least approximate to the correct one as the skipper can see the sea ahead of him. Possibly the 'navigator' has already worked out the reciprocal of the course in the pilot book by adding, or subtracting, 180 degrees. In any event, even if the course is approximately correct, it is highly unlikely to serve, because neither variation nor deviation have been applied to it. Unless the variation and deviation cancel one another out by being equal and opposite, the course offered is NOT the course to steer.

Furthermore, the skipper is taking no account of any cross-sets which may be affecting him. He should be arranging a back bearing on a conspicuous point that was dead astern as he began this leg of his pilotage. Better still, he should have observed a suitable transit. A transit need not be an 'official' one. A tree and a parked car would be fine, or perhaps the lefthand edge of a field of rape in line with a dip in the hills, or even a stationary cow and a nuclear power station.

What the skipper must not do on any account is simply steer a compass course (even if it is ostensibly the correct one, which this isn't!) in a situation where dangers are close at hand. The course to steer is only the starting point, after that he must use his eyes and, if necessary, his echo sounder to ensure that his boat remains on the safe track his course to steer originally denoted.

This crew will be more fortunate than they deserve, if all remains peace on board.   TC

Tom's solution is substantially the same as mine for the tacking problem. In part ii he makes a mildly contentious point regarding bearings given in pilot books which makes my question slightly shaky, but basically the same truth emerges.

When a boat sails fast over such shallow water a drag is set up (smelling the bottom), a suction effect which can affect steering to a serious extent and the faster she sails the more pronounced the effect. Perhaps they diagnosed this as the problem and spilled wind to slow the boat; she would then have been more likely to tack. Or perhaps they let go their anchor again, which would have been ready having only just been hauled in, and by so doing snubbed her bows round in the classic manoeuvre.

As for that bearing of 210 degrees, since it was taken straight from the pilot book rather than plotted on the chart the odds are that it was a True bearing, which should have been converted to a compass heading.   JDS

PART TWO

They had no compass and there was no sight of the sun to guide them . . .

A nice day's fishing

Yachtsmen and their misadventures come in for a good deal of stick in the media when they have to be rescued from their follies, but sea anglers account for a large share of rescue missions and all too often it is because their boats and equipment fall far short of the ideal. To an angler a boat is a 'fishing platform' and bare of anything much beyond bait and beer. Thus it was with the two anglers who took their 18ft outboard dory four miles offshore one dull day in November.

But the fish were biting and they were in an angler's heaven as they hauled in the codling. Their lunch went untouched as fish followed fish and even when the drizzle began their fervour remained undiminished. It was not until their catch began to dwindle that they began to take note of their surroundings. The low-lying coastline had vanished from view and so had all other objects around them, they lay to their anchor in a sombre grey void, moreover the short winter day was fading into dusk. They had no compass and there was no sight of the sun to guide them. Presumably as the boat was pointing into the tidal current, which ran roughly north–south along the coast the land lay to the west, to starboard.

'Here's a rum go' said one, 'The land's over there mate but once we haul our anchor up and the boat's drifting we won't know which way she's pointing will we?'

The tide was nearly done and soon she wouldn't even be pointing into the current, something had to be done but what? How would they know that they weren't simply motoring out to sea or along the coast? What might they try?   JDS

The anglers have two problems to tackle: what direction to go and, once under way, how to maintain their heading. At the moment their only point of reference is the tide yet that too is soon to turn. As darkness isn't

going to make things worse — in fact it may ease the problem as shore lights will help them as they close the coast — they would do better to sit tight for a couple of hours until they can be certain the tide has turned so their reference point is going to remain constant for some hours.

If they were really resourceful they might straighten out one of their larger fish hooks, magnetise it on their outboard's magneto and then dangle it on a length of fishing line as a makeshift compass but for the sake of this exercise we'll rule that one out. If there's any wind at all it will create another reference point, waves, that will give them a way to maintain heading. The wind itself, if light, will only give a little help once under way and the direction of movement of the clouds, if visible, is another clue. Armed with these they probably don't have quite enough information to weigh anchor and head inshore with any confidence. One thing they have got on board is their fishing tackle.

If they tie a heavy weight to the end of one of their lines and allow it to drag along the bottom and motor ahead at just a couple of knots this line will be angled out to one side because of the stream. All they need to do is to leave engine speed constant and maintain the angle of the line, their tide compass. If in doubt they can re-anchor to check the direction of the stream and set off again. The angle of the line may change as tidal rate changes but as long as they keep the angle open on the same side of the boat they will be heading towards land. AB

―――――

Apart from being prize idiots in venturing offshore in winter without a compass there was one trick that might work since all they needed was to be able to close the coast — and they had the necessary equipment in profusion. Andrew has spotted it.

They had their fishing lines. By streaming a line astern while motoring along the boat can be kept in a reasonably straight line by keeping the line dead centre astern. First though they must stream a line, suitably lightened of weights, astern in the tideway as they lay at anchor. Then, having hauled in their anchor they motor ahead to leave a wake. By turning 90 degrees towards the shore and streaming a second line while the first is hauled in a shorewards heading is established. The rest then depends upon the consumption of canned beer earlier on. Andrew Bray's answer shows that there are two ways to kill the same cat.   JDS

Choice of two evils

Fred had agreed to go on the cross-Channel passage to give an inexperienced owner confidence in his new boat and this would be her maiden passage. The boat was a 30-footer of conventional but wholesome design with a good though basic inventory and her new owner had but one season of experience behind him, the third hand was a youngster with no offshore experience but he was fit and an active windsurfer.

The weather forecast was unremarkable, a trough was moving in from the west and expected to give showers and force 4–5 south westerlies, locally force 6 and moderating later. On a course of 175 degrees magnetic this meant a close fetch, none too comfortable but a good test of a new boat and her crew. Of course it didn't pan out that way, these things seldom do. For the first four hours there was no wind at all and they motored along sedately, then the engine began to labour. It seemed to Fred most likely that they had caught something around the prop, plastic sheeting perhaps, but the owner, who was never happier than when he was tinkering with an engine, thought otherwise and he was soon down below busily stripping the engine.

Fortunately a little breeze arrived from the south west so that they could at least sail the course, but the sky had become overcast and it began to drizzle and a swell was building up. The owner suddenly appeared on deck looking very green and made for the lee rail. He went below again, reassembled the engine and took to his bunk without another word. Needless to say, the engine when started showed no sign of improvement and Fred shut it off. The youngster was all for going overboard with a knife between his teeth but it was still early in the season and Fred knew that the sea would be very cold so he refused the offer.

By the afternoon shipping forecast time the yacht had reached the point of no return, exactly halfway, 30 miles out and 30 to go. The forecast had a nasty surprise. The trough, it seemed, had developed into a small but active low and a southerly gale was imminent with deteriorating visibility. The low was tracking north of them and conditions were expected to improve quite quickly, meanwhile the prospect of beating into a rising gale was daunting, the yacht was untried, one member of the crew was already *hors de combat* and the other member was an unknown quantity, added to all this the engine could at best give them four knots in calm water.

Fred reviewed the options. Had the engine been unimpaired and giving its potential six or more knots it might have been possible to bash hard to windward for as long as possible in the hope of getting at least some protection from the distant weather shore before the gale reached them. He could still sail hard while they could and then heave to. The yacht's mainsail could be rolled down pretty small but the owner had not yet got around to equipping her with a small storm jib although she had a small working jib. It was a summer gale warning not a severe storm warning and they could therefore expect force 8 squalling to 9 perhaps which they should be able to handle under mainsail only if needs be. The problem with heaving to, Fred thought, was that they'd by then be in the vicinity of the busy shipping lanes.

The alternative was to cut and run now. They could make six maybe seven knots and be back off their home coast in four or five hours. It was no easy choice for Fred but the prospect of struggling to windward, perhaps single handed, dismayed him, back they would go. Do you agree with his decision?   JDS

The immediate outlook may be a little bleak but the heartening feature of this situation is that things are going to get better before too long.

The key to taking the right decision is an accurate assessment of the speed of the depression. As it passes to the north the wind is going to veer westerly and eventually north westerly. The wind will fill in and strengthen from the south before it starts to veer but as it starts to swing to the west it will become as easy to continue to the south as to return to the north.

The snag with Fred's decision to turn and run is that he is heading for a lee shore, a situation which could be difficult if he arrives off the coast when the sea has had a few hours to build up. It will be even worse if the wind veers north of west and he is left with a beat through a confused and irregular sea.

If he had decided to keep going the immediate prospect would indeed have been bleak but there are two points in favour of continuing south. At first he may make only modest progress, probably no more than three knots but as the wind starts to veer the rate of progress is going to improve. An important factor is going to be the morale of his younger crewman. The youngster is likely to equate turning back with giving up.

Is there actually much more danger in going on than there is in turning back? Whichever option Fred chooses he is not going to reach harbour before the gale arrives. If he turns back he is foresaking the shelter (however slight) of a weather shore but he is keeping out of the shipping lane and he is almost certainly shortening the time at sea. If he continues he is going to have less difficulty keeping his remaining fit crewman happy and I suspect that his own morale will be higher because the worst of the passage will be over more quickly.

How happy is Fred going to be in 12 hours time? By then he is going to be in harbour and it is usually more fun to be in a foreign port.   BA

―――――――

Assuming that it blows a gale, and there is no certainty of this, the classification 'imminent' means that it is expected to develop within three hours from the time of broadcast and visibility in that case would decrease dramatically. If they turn back it would probably mean that they would be running towards a lee shore in thick weather and with a gale astern, a chilling thought at the best of times and as Fred would have to navigate with extreme care and accuracy who would be sailing the boat? Even if the owner could be bullied into taking the helm would he be trustworthy? Certainly the total beginner however keen would not be up to it.

On the other hand however hectic it might be to continue sailing to windward and later perhaps heaving to the danger would be considerably less, even if they hove to near a shipping lane. The wind would be unlikely to stay in the same quarter for long, it would either back further or veer and either way this should give them a better chance to make up under the land and they would feel the benefit of it ten or fifteen miles from it. A wind shift off a lee shore would still leave it a highly dangerous position to be in. Pressing on would be the safer option. Bill seems to agree.   JDS

Three men in a boat, minus two

The *Golden Garbler* is an old-fashioned 28ft bermudan cutter. She sails well enough but, unlike many more modern vessels, she will not sail upwind satisfactorily on her headsails alone. Her crew consists of Jake the skipper, Victor his mate, and Jake's cousin Willy, who is a competent dinghy sailor and is now trying to run up the miles for his Yachtmaster's ticket.

The weather is moderate and the boys are enjoying a fine broad reach through a choppy sea thrown up by a strong weather-going tide. Willy is at the helm and Jake is below washing up the lunch dishes when Victor elects to obey nature's call in the traditional way at the pushpit. Willy politely averts his gaze and doesn't see Victor as with a particularly awkward lurch, the *Golden Garbler* heaves him over the side. Victor swallows a mouthful of sea as he hits the drink and it is several seconds before he has finished spluttering and gathered his wits for the shout. By now, the *Garbler* is well down wind.

After hearing Victor's wail, Willy freezes for a few seconds, then yells for Jake. The skipper comes up on deck, makes a rapid assessment of the situation, marks Victor by transiting him with a tree and a hilltop on the distant shore and takes the helm.

'Get up forward, Willy,' he orders calmly, 'and drop the headsails.' As Willy moves to the mast, Jake starts the engine and puts it slow ahead, bringing the boat to the wind as he does so. Willy dramatically throws down the coil of what he thinks is the jib halyard and casts it off the cleat, but he's made a bad mistake and chosen the wrong halyard. Just as the mainsail starts tumbling down the track Willy trips and kicks the fall of the halyard over the side where it is immediately grabbed by the propeller. As the rope winds around the shaft, the mainsail shoots back up to the masthead and just before the engine stops, the headboard is ripped out of the sail, which rattles down again. Jake has always made a point of sailing with plenty of slack in the topping lift and now, relieved of the supporting sail, the heavy boom crashes down onto his head like a pile-driver.

Willy watches with horror as Jake crumples unconscious to the cockpit sole under a heap of sail and rope. Two hundred yards up to windward Victor is occasionally visible as he bobs up to a wave-top. The old cutter's head has by now fallen off the wind as the engine jerks to its terminal halt and she is now lying, headsails aback, with the wind abaft the starboard beam.

An unknown voice once heard in the club bar is echoing through the back of Willy's brain, 'If you can sail one boat, you can sail 'em all,' it had said with fruity confidence. The picture of his Enterprise capsizing yet again flashes into the memory slot in place of the voice and Willy realises he's not so sure. There was nothing on his Coastal Skipper practical course to cover this situation. But he must do something to help his friends.

The question is, 'what?'   TC

Poor cousin Willy, he's faced with a nearly impossible situation. But his dinghy sailing skills and Coastal Skipper practical experience could just be enough to give him and Victor a chance, provided he stays calm and lets his common sense prevail. The engine avenue of escape is obviously firmly closed as are any options that are going to take more than a couple of minutes. Although Jake may be badly hurt, Victor has to be his priority because unless he can get the Golden Garbler back to him he has no chance of survival.

So his first action, if he has not done so already, is to launch a lifebuoy, with dan buoy if it has one. It should drift off downwind close enough for Victor to swim across to it. If successful he's bought time to consider the next problem — Jake. If he's very badly hurt there's not much Willy will be able to do. All he should do at this stage is to staunch any bad bleeding and move him as little as possible to somewhere he is secure and clear of the essential controls of the boat — tiller and sheets.

Lowering the foresail will help to reduce drift away from Victor but he should leave the staysail as he'll need it if he's to sail to windward. Next he should turn his attention to the main. What are his options to re-hoist without a headboard and halyard? The topping lift is his only chance. If he takes the first three of four slides out of the track and ties an overhand knot in the head of the sail he can make fast the topping lift with a rolling hitch below the knot. All the time he should be watching Victor — hopefully at one with the lifebuoy — to note his position. He is now in a position to re-hoist. The main won't exactly be pretty but it should provide enough power together with the staysail to go to windward. And his dinghy experience should be more than enough to allow him to tack back towards Victor and finish up to weather of him either hove to or with all sheets freed. He might also contemplate lowering his jury main leaving Golden Gauntlet lying quietly with staysail aback whilst Victor swims over to her and with a little help climbs back on board. Once Victor is below and wrapped in a sleeping bag he can turn his attention to Jake.   AB

———

Cousin Willy has done all the right things here. His order of priorities is sensible, and he is a bright lad to realise that an injured sail can sometimes be hoisted in the way he has contrived. My only difference with him is that, as I perceive the situation, the boat was somewhat downwind of Victor when the traumatic events took place, in the cockpit and around the propeller shaft. If that were so, Victor would never get near the lifebuoy. Even so, Willy's policy of keeping an eye on Victor at all times may still save the day.

The young fellow has also done everything he reasonably could for his skipper. Maybe Victor will prove to be a medical practitioner who can sort Jake out. I have every confidence that with a man of Willy's calibre in charge, Victor will soon be back aboard.　　TC

Hook, line and sinker

'Must have been very hungry,' said Geoff, inspecting the frayed end of the Walker log line. And always the joker 'what do you reckon he was, great white or killer whale?'

A spare spinner for the Walker had been on the list of Things to Do before we left six days earlier. But after being gale bound for five days the prospect of the promised moderate north westerlies had seemed more important at the start of what was going to be our first ocean cruise, bound for Horta in the Azores. But as the Walker itself was a back up for the through hull log I had thought we were well enough covered. I hadn't reckoned with the flotsam that knocked off its impeller on our second day out, nor with predatory fish.

'Columbus made it without a log,' joked Geoff, 'so with your high tech navigation it shouldn't be a problem.' High tech it might have been when still enmeshed in the Decca lattice and within range of radio beacons, but with the nearest land 250 miles to port and 600 to go to our destination the electronic navigation cupboard was decidedly bare. And anyway, Columbus had a somewhat larger target to head for. By comparison the Azores were mere dots on the ocean and if we missed, South America the next stop.

I went down to the chart table to review the situation. The accuracy of my sun sights had improved enormously since leaving though without a log to measure distance run between sights this would become a guessing game. And could such logless navigation be accurate enough to get within RDF range of the beacons on the Azores? I had yet to graduate to star sights. There was one obvious, if slightly hit and miss, solution. But then as I ran through the workings of my morning sight again another answer suggested itself, so blindingly simple that I had to check it a second time to make sure. And it could be as accurate as my astro navigation allowed. All I had to do was . . . and what was the first, hit and miss solution? AB

The lack of a log need not be a problem— as long as the sun continues to shine. All you have to do is plan your sights intelligently.

Assume that your course towards Horta is 220 degrees. At some time during the forenoon the sun is going to be on your port beam. If you take a sight at that time, the resulting position line will tell you whether you are to port or starboard of your planned track.

During the afternoon you can take the second sight of the day, when the sun is directly ahead. This time the plotted position line will tell you exactly how far it is to your destination.

These two single position line sights give you all the information you need, you can even run the first up to the second, if it makes you feel more comfortable to have a cross on the chart, although you are not actually finding out any more about your position by doing so. Just think in terms of knowing whether you are left or right of the planned track during the morning and how far you have to go during the afternoon.

With 600 miles to go you need something to occupy the time so why not make up a proper old fashioned log — with knots in it? The essential materials are a fishing line, an old dish cloth and a tape measure (or an exact knowledge of the span of the outstretched arms of one of the crew).

Use the dish cloth for the outer end of the line and tie the knots 50.6ft apart if you are going to use half-minute timings or 25.3ft apart for 15 second timings. If you take the mean of five speed measurements twice an hour you will not only be able to take 'sun run sun' sights, by the time you reach Horta you will have become expert at estimating the speed of the yacht. Which is just as well because by then the dish cloth will have disintegrated. BA

Bill's answer is a very practical and straightforward solution to the problem which would, if not actually hit Horta on the nose, bring him within easy visual or RDF range of the high Azores islands.

My own solution is a variation on the theme suggested and it was one that worked for me when I was in exactly in this situation between the West Coast of England and the Azores. For the first two days I used 'sun run sun' using a chip log to estimate speed and hence distance travelled between sights. The 'chip log' method involves throwing a small piece of wood (the chip) over the bow and then timing it along the known length of the boat to estimate speed. It was on day three that I had The Revelation. I noticed just how close the Position Line (LOP) from my morning sight was to the course I was steering. By working a sight backwards, using course steered as the LOP until I arrived at a time to take a sight I established exactly when I should shoot the sun so as to be able to 'sail down' the morning sight LOP, later crossing this with an afternoon sight to obtain an accurate position. In practice a minor course correction was all that was necessary to allow for the actual time of the sight.

The other method I referred to as being 'hit and miss' is simpler. By taking noon sights I could sail south until on the latitude of Horta and then just by sailing west — and checking latitude daily with a noon sight I could 'run down my westing' with a fair chance of seeing the island before hitting it! AB

Tonight Josephine?

The daylight was just beginning to die as the 55ft cutter, *Gulliver*, beat up the last three miles to Jewel Island off the coast of Maine. The smoky sou'westerly which had been blowing since morning was piping up nastily, raising the anxiety level of Napoleon, the skipper, along with an ugly, white-capped sea.

Neither Napoleon nor his two crewmen had ever visited Jewel before, but the 34ft *Voice of Reason* with whom they seemed to have joined up had called there every summer for the past ten years. Last night as the two yachts rafted up in a sheltered cove further along the coast towards Canada, the other boat's owner, Josephine, had advised Napoleon and his mates about the sterling qualities of Jewel Island's anchorage. Shelter from all weather was assured, and the promise of a quiet night was made even more alluring to the three men as they thought of Josephine and her beautiful daughters, already in there perhaps, and waiting for them.

The VHF crackled into life.

'*Gulliver*, this is the *Voice of Reason*.'

'*Voice of Reason*; *Gulliver*. Go ahead on Channel 6.'

'Good evening, *Gulliver*. We've anchored now; right on the inside. We thought we'd better warn you the place is a bit crowded. The Lilliputian Sailing Club is here *en masse* on their annual cruise, but there's room for you up near to us. We've put supper on for you, so don't you be long, now.'

'Roger, *Voice of Reason*. We'll be half an hour, maybe. So keep the champagne on ice. *Gulliver* out.' Napoleon's hopes for the evening soared as he thought of the way Josephine had smiled at him from beneath lowered eyelids the previous evening. He inspected the chart for a minute or two, then pranced up to the deck.

'Right, boys,' he said in his most authoritative tone. 'Sails down; let's be sure to get in before dark.'

Défarge and Talleyrand leapt to it and in next to no time *Gulliver* was snugged down and motoring steadily into the hidden anchorage. The sight that greeted them as they rounded the final corner was enough to daunt the bravest. The long, narrow harbour appeared to be 'wall-to-wall' boats, none of them over 25ft long. Down at the bottom end, as Josephine had promised, the tall mast of the *Voice of Reason* rose serenely above the mob, like a slender, beckoning finger.

Just for a moment the thought flashed through Napoleon's computer-like brain that maybe Josephine had been guilty of a modicum of wishful thinking when she had said that there was room for *Gulliver*, but not being a man to give up easily on a promising situation, he took a deep breath and plunged in.

As *Gulliver* threaded her way delicately through the Lilliputians she narrowly missed one boat after another as they surged about on their nylon anchor rodes in the rising wind.

'Get that great thing outa here!' bawled one of the Lilliput men. 'What the hell is this guy trying to prove!'

Up on *Gulliver's* foredeck, Talleyrand was preparing the 70lb plough anchor while Défarge shackled up the $\frac{7}{16}$ chain bower cable. Napoleon meanwhile was working out how little scope he dare allow, bearing in mind that there was effectively no tide. The cove was surrounded by rocks on all sides. The holding ground was given in the pilot book as fair, but not marvellous and, as Napoleon could now see clearly, he wasn't going to have more than four or five boats' lengths swinging room at the end. The chart suggested that he would be anchoring in 15ft of water if he were half a cable from the blind end of the harbour, but he needed to be closer than that because of the Lilliputians, and also, the *Voice of Reason* herself, which he could now see swinging to her rode, the last boat in the crowd.

At the moment, the wind was coming directly over the trees at the root of the harbour, but it was forecast to veer through 180 degrees during the night.

Napoleon switched on his echo sounder and viewed the battlefield, thinking of his 8ft draught. It was blowing hard now and just beginning to rain. The little boats were surging around like mad things and he asked himself what his insurers would say if he

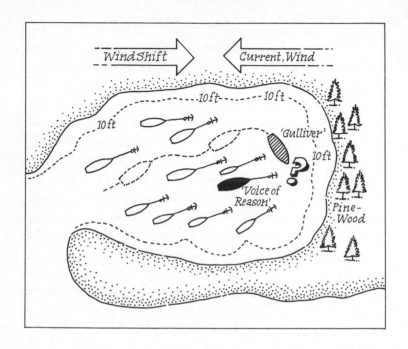

anchored in that tiny hole and then came into collision with one or more of them during the night. For a few moments he seriously considered going back out again in spite of the weather, but just then, Josephine came up on deck carrying the riding light, her long hair free and blowing in the wind. As she raised her arms gracefully to attach the lamp to the forestay, his heart skipped a beat and his hormones took over from his judgement. By now he was entering the patch of clear water in which he needed to lie and he was able to assess matters on the spot. *Gulliver* had every item he had been able to think of when it came to ground tackle, but even so it was going to be, as Wellington once remarked, 'a damned nice thing.'

How can Napoleon and his men safely arrange matters so as to be confident of an undisturbed night? TC

———

One thing to be sure of is that Gulliver's *ground tackle is as near bullet proof as the holding ground will permit. But although he could motor*

slowly ahead and drop his hook in 10ft before easing back, he clearly hasn't the swinging room when the expected veer occurs. If he anchors further back to lie close ahead of Voice of Reason *and the nearest Lilliputian, with 60 feet of cable out and his own 55 feet of length he still stands the risk of going ashore with the change of wind. He can't afford to drop back between the two as both will be dancing around on their nylon rodes while he'll lie steadier to his heavy chain cable. But there is just one option open to him if it's not to be 'not tonight, Napoleon'.*

His boys, though, are going to have to work hard for their supper. To start with he's going to anchor on very short scope – perhaps initially just 2:1, holding her against the wind with the engine – between and very close ahead of Voice of Reason *and the Lilliputian. Défarge and Talleyrand now take to the dinghy and row a heavy warp ashore and make it fast around the largest and most convenient of the pine trees. Once they are back on board Napoleon motors slow ahead, turning* Gulliver *whilst the boys haul in the warp at the stern until she is lying stern to the wind. Napoleon veers more cable until he has 4:1 scope and his stern will now be in about 10 feet of water – plenty as the anchorage is non tidal. As the wind veers the other yachts should swing clear of him. After taking in the slack on the stern warp he should take one last precaution. There will be one point during the night when he'll be lying beam onto the wind and liable to drag. A kedge laid well out from his bows at 90 degrees in the direction of the veer should hold him there for the night. The evening's promised delights, though, are likely to be interrupted. Because if anything starts to drag he could have very real problems on his hands so he owes it to himself and his insurers to stand anchor watches.* AB

I'm glad to see Napoleon is going to take the field. Andrew's solution to his dilemma is the same as mine in all things except for the matter of how he puts *Gulliver* into the chosen moored state. Andrew's system will work. Here is an alternative suggestion:

Napoleon motors ahead into the shallow water just under the trees, then launches the dinghy with Talleyrand and Défarge. He stooges around while they attach the warp to the trees and come back aboard. Once they have regained the deck, the warp is led over the stern and *Gulliver* motors away to where the anchor is to be laid, paying out slack as she goes. The anchor is then dropped and *Gulliver*'s stern is kept 'up' to the wind by using the warp. She is then motored astern with Défarge gathering slack on the warp and controlling her swinging as necessary, while Talleyrand, 'on foredeck winch', surges anchor cable to taste. Once *Gulliver* is lying in her chosen 10ft, the anchor cable is hardened in until Napoleon is sure the hook is well set. He can then ease out a fathom or two and lie to the catenary of his manly chain cable.

It's a smart move to lay the kedge. Napoleon hadn't thought of that. If I were him, as a final refinement, I'd bribe Défarge and Talleyrand with promises of lesser kingships in return for being excused anchor watch duties!   TC

Familiarity breeds

The Caribbean is not, as often fondly supposed, a sea of gentle breezes, calm waters and waving palms. The seas that reach the islands in the Windward group have travelled without hindrance for 4000 miles and are full blooded ocean swells, heightened as they are squeezed between the islands. The winds, the reliable easterly to north easterly Trades behave likewise. Typically force 5 but often 6 or more, they too accelerate in the inter island passes and give unpredictable squalls, especially at the headlands.

As the islands lie roughly north/south these Trades allow for very fast and lively passage making, beam reaching down and beam reaching back again. For the two of us it was as regular as the daily commuter train. We had been working charter boats for a long season and now it was time to re-fit our own boat, left afloat but laid up in Martinique for some months now. We had hitched a lift up from our charter base in Rodney Bay, St Lucia where we planned to return with the boat, a 35ft catamaran that had taken us safely for many thousands of miles of blue water cruising.

It was to have been just another routine trip of just a few hours. Most of the gear had been stripped off her and was safely stored at Rodney Bay and we had travelled lightly — just a couple of packs of sandwiches and a dozen cans of beer to sustain us for what should have been at most a six hour passage. We were now in a situation entirely of our own making.

As we had rounded the southern tip of Martinique, carrying full sail, a squall had screamed down on us and before we'd had the chance even to free sheets there was a loud crack as a cap shroud parted and the mast gracefully fell over the side. We had fuel enough for at most half an hour's motoring, no stores, no water, no charts and apart from compass and log no navigational instruments. The VHF aerial had disappeared along with the mast but we did have some flares on board — though there was little chance of their being seen. Even if we were able to set up a jury rig, at the best of times the catamaran was not fleet to windward. The combination of the strong Trades and the 2 knot west going Equatorial current made it highly unlikely that we could make any progress to windward under jury rig. Downwind the nearest land was Venezuela, some 240 miles away. What options are open to us?   AB

————

The first, essential, job is to clear away the wreckage of the mast. You need to get rid of it quicky before it adds to your problems by punching a hole in a hull but don't be too ready to attack the remaining shrouds with a pair of bolt-croppers. Get as much gear as you can back on board, it may be useful for a jury rig.

Having made sure that the boat is as safe as possible, I don't think there is a 'right' answer that is going to solve your problem. There are, however, a number of things you can do, any of which might help to save your life and your boat.

Anchoring is almost certainly out of the question. The passages

between the islands are deep, mostly well over 100 fathoms and it is highly unlikely that you have enough length of cable, warps, sheets and halyards on board even to reach the sea bed.

The closer you can get to land, the better the chance of someone seeing you. Start the engine and head for the nearest island, which will probably be Martinique. As soon as the boat is on course start sorting out gear for a jury rig.

With any luck you will make three or four miles before the fuel runs out. Now is the time to use two of your flares, because this may be the closest that you are ever going to get to land. Don't be tempted to use them all, they may not be seen and in a few hours time you may see a passing ship — it would be heart-breaking not to be able to signal to her.

The next move must be to try to set up a jury rig. Although catamarans are not at their best to windward they do close reach well and if you can improvise a sail that will give you four knots, 60 degrees off the wind, you will be able to hold ground to windward against the two knot current. This is by no means an impossible aim in a force 5–6.

If you have not been rescued, or made land, by dark it may be worth using another couple of flares. If the shore lights are visible then your flares will also be visible, although whether or not anyone actually sees them is, of course, largely a matter of chance.

In spite of all your efforts you may fail to make contact with an island. In that case your only hope is to head south west, as fast as you can. A combination of the favourable current and jury rig should allow you to make at least 80 miles a day and a can of beer a day should be ample to sustain life and a certain amount of strength. You won't need any food for the first two days and by then the prospect of a stale sandwich will be surprisingly welcome.

What are you going to do when you reach land? Having made it that far I suspect that you will manage the final stage without further gratuitous advice!   BA

———

I wouldn't argue with a single point Bill has made but would venture just two possible observations. Although the VHF aerial went over the side with the mast, it should be possible to salvage it and rig it on a boathook or even the boom before drifting out of VHF range. VHF in the Caribbean is widely used by charter boats as a chat line and there would be a fair chance of a call being picked up and hopefully acted on. The second point assuming all else has failed and the crew are resigning themselves to a long slow trip to Venezuela is that short but very heavy tropical downpurs are common in the Caribbean. They should, as soon as a jury rig is set up and working turn their minds to the problem of water catchment. The catamaran has enormous deck space and if they are successful could probably even have enough to wash with.   AB

Sleigh ride

'Feeling brave, skipper? Do you want the spinnaker as soon as we're round Rame Head? The gear's all rigged and the wind will be right astern.'

Nick considered John's question. He was right about the wind direction, it would be astern on the leg to Falmouth. The spinnaker would help to steady her in the swell. But with only three of them on board the big masthead spinnaker on the 40-footer would not be easy to handle in the force 5.

'No thanks John,' Nick answered. 'We'll settle for booming out the headsail. It won't be much slower and it will be a lot less hassle. Would you like to get the pole ready on the port side.'

'I'd rather wait until we're round the head,' John replied. 'The foredeck should be dry when we bear away.'

Ten minutes later they were squared away onto a dead run. John eased the starboard headsail sheet and hauled on the port one to goosewing the genoa.

'I should leave it on the starboard side for the moment.' Nick suggested. 'It will be much easier to set up the pole with a topping lift and foreguy with the port headsail sheet through the jaws and then haul the clew out to the pole.'

'That sounds a bit complicated,' said John. 'If I goosewing it first all I have to do on the foredeck is clip the outer end of the pole to the sheet or the clew of the sail, shove it out and clip the inboard end to the mast. The foot of that genoa's so long that I won't even have to shove it out with the pole.'

'You've both got it wrong,' chipped in Brian, who had been listening with interest. 'I agree with John that Nick's system is unnecessarily complicated but it would certainly be easier to rig the pole on a lazy sheet before you goosewing the genoa.'

'I'm sure you're both experts at booming out headsails,' said Nick 'But could we get on with it or we'll be in Falmouth before we get the boom rigged. And since she's my boat could we do it my way?'

Which way would you have boomed out the headsail?   BA

––––––––

John's suggestion might work on a small boat but on a 40-footer with a force 5 following wind and a large genoa there is just too much to go wrong on a rolling foredeck. It just needs the genoa to back momentarily when the pole is clipped onto the sheet but before it is on the mast to have John over the side, impaled by the pole or worse.

The pole on a boat of this size could be nearly 20 feet long and none too light either. Handling it manually could easily lead to an unwelcome and intimate acquaintance with it. Nick's suggestion has some merit in that the pole is set up before any load is on it but suffers one drawback. To 'haul the clew out', as he suggests, will be none too easy and could cause damage to the pole and its fittings as the sail fills as it is hauled across. The best solution is going to be a compromise between Nick's and Brian's methods. The genoa should be allowed to goose wing and a lazy sheet rigged. The pole can now be set up with topping lift and foreguy but with this lazy sheet through the jaws. It is then just a simple matter of transferring the load from the sheet to the lazy sheet. It may take a few minutes but with the 30-odd miles to Falmouth to sail, it's worth having it properly set up in the first place.   AB

Yes. If the spinnaker boom is set up with a topping lift, foreguy and after guy it will be under total control. The trouble taken to rig the three lines will be well worth it, particularly if the wind increases. Trying to hook the outboard end of the boom to the clew and then the inboard end to the mast involves a highly dangerous dance with death on the foredeck! Definitely not recommended.   BA

Just coasting

It was really just a delivery trip, the first passage of the season from the creek where she'd been laid up to the home river ten miles down the coast and they knew every yard of the way. It was a calm, warm morning of pearly, hazy sunshine and they droned along under engine two miles offshore more absorbed in their conversation than with the navigation. Anyway, no chart was needed and neither was a compass course, they just followed parallel to the coast.

Then, without anybody noticing, the coast just disappeared and the buoy astern to port vanished too and by the time they became aware of it the pearly haze had become an extensive fog bank. They weren't much worried, they had recently passed the East Gant buoy and the helmsman noted his compass heading and began steering to it. They switched on the echo sounder and continued at their steady three knots while the skipper spread the chart and began, belatedly perhaps, to navigate.

The seabed was relatively flat thereabouts and therefore not much help, neither was the RDF because the nearest useful beacons were at almost maximum range and gave a poor cross anyway. He put an approximate position on the chart though and began looking for the tidal information. Then he remembered that the new tables were still at home. The stream was foul though, he was sure of that but how foul and for how long he couldn't guess. Then he had an idea, on this heading they would be crossing the mouth of a river and the soundings would increase and then decrease again as they crossed the deeper water, on their present heading they had only to do a log run between changes of sounding and they would be able to estimate the tidal rate. The stretch of deeper water on their course would be near enough half a mile.

It all worked out as expected, half an hour later the echo sounder took a dive and they checked the log. It took ten minutes to cross the deeper water which at three knots meant half a mile and therefore no current against them. It must be slack water. Odd, the skipper thought, he shrugged and began considering the next step. He studied the chart, there was another one and a half miles to steam on this course and then they must alter course straight inshore and watch the 'sounder. They should be cutting obliquely across the edge of their home river channel and having found it they then had only to follow in on the soundings.

The fog eddied and swirled but they were safe from shipping, there were no rocks or shoals along their track and this early in the season there were unlikely to be any other yachts to pose a collision risk. They broke open another six-pack of beers and droned on their way. Half an hour later the skipper looked at the log and ordered a change of course. Slowing a little they motored inshore, all eyes on the echo sounder. Minutes passed, the soundings decreased steadily. 'Any moment now' somebody said. But still there was no sign of the deeper water which would indicate their channel.

Suddenly everyone yelped out in alarm as the soundings decreased from a comfortable five metres to three . . . two . . . and BUMP! What could possibly have gone wrong?   JDS

What could possibly have gone wrong? The skipper, that's what. He made a thorough dog's breakfast of a comparatively simple piece of blind navigation.

In the first place it was crass to assume that if he steered what he imagined might be a straight course from East Gant, he would arrive at the first river channel two miles further on at exactly the spot he marked so

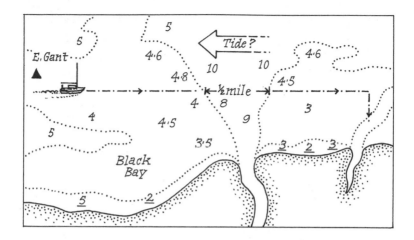

optimistically on his chart. The tide, he was confident, was foul. He had just passed East Gant so presumably he noted the stream flowing around the buoy. If he didn't, he should have done, particularly in the absence of tide tables.

When stemming a foul tide, a small discrepancy in course steered will generate a disproportionate lateral displacement of the boat from her planned track, while if the tidal stream is anything other than the exact reciprocal of the boat's course, she will be set to one side in any case.

In this instance she was obviously set inshore. She ran a half mile through the deeper water and this, taking into consideration the foul tide, must have placed her somewhere inshore of where the skipper thought he was. Where, exactly, doesn't actually matter; because even if he had known what the predicted stream was, he would still have been unwise to stick slavishly to the normal 'full vision' navigation of dead reckoning, estimated position, and course shaping direct for a destination.

What he should have done when he knew he'd passed the first river exit was offer thanks, because that meant he had at least an approximae East–West position.

Unfortunately, instead of settling for this, he fell into the oldest trap of all and forced the evidence to fit in with his conclusions, rather than vice versa. He ran a half mile and, had he been on his track and had there been no tide running, this distance would have fixed his position as shown in the *illustration and according to his plan. He liked the sound of that, so he ignored his strong suspicion that there was a foul tide running and swept the idea out of the way under the chart table. That was his cardinal sin.*

With the wisdom of hindsight we can see that he was wrong. The tide was, of course, foul; he was doomed to failure before ever he began his final approach and he ran ashore somewhere to the west of the home river.

What he should have done is this: as soon as he had passed over the deep water of the first river mouth, he knew he was somewhere on the 5m contour to the east of it. He should then have shaped an approximate course that he was certain, whatever the rate or direction of the tide, would place him inshore of his current position and west of the entrance to the home river. He would follow this course, say, as far as the 2m line as measured on his echo sounder. (If his yacht were of deep draught he would opt for more water.)

Once he had carefully found this contour, it only remained to run it to the eastward until the suddenly increasing depth on an easterly heading showed him that he had found the river mouth. He would then have turned southward to follow the deep water in, keeping to, say, the 2m or 3m line on the righthand bank.

The illustration shows clearly that had the skipper adopted these tactics, the tidal current assessment would be irrelevant to a safe arrival. At no time until he entered home river would he have known exactly where he was, but this would not have mattered. He would have been following a simple and foolproof plan which could have had no other result than to bring him home rejoicing.   TC

All might have worked out well had their track been where they thought it was. In fact they *did* have a foul stream against them and as so often happens there was a strong inset into Black Bay and by the time they had reached the river they were crossing a narrower stretch of deeper water, only a quarter mile wide instead of their estimated half mile, thus it was that their ten minutes at three knots should have indicated that they had one and a half knots of stream against them. The rest of the story needs no explanation, they under-ran their distance against that unsuspected foul tide and when they made their course alteration it took them straight up the beach. Tom Cunliffe propounds a good solution.   JDS

The Dutch dilemma

The approach to Vannes in the upper reaches of the Morbihan twists and turns through the picturesque Conleau narrows before opening up to a wide expanse of water where the channel is marked with a series of withies. A final hard turn to port and Vannes lies ahead at the end of a long narrow canal, the marina situated right in the heart of this attractive and bustling French city. Accessible for just a few hours each tide, the basin is protected by a single lock gate which is closed three hours or so after HW to maintain a 2.4m depth inside.

Hans was a careful navigator and seaman and this was reflected in the thoroughly workmanlike appearance of *Matilde*, 15 tons of best Dutch steel and 40 feet in length, though with a draught of 7 feet hardly the ideal boat for these waters. Her equipment too was solid and more than adequate to deal with her heavy gear, from her hydraulic windlass to the 75hp Perkins now murmuring quietly below the cockpit sole as he conned her the last few hundred yards towards the lock gates.

With HW Vannes two hours later than at Port Navalo at the entrance to the Morbihan it is, in theory, possible to enter the harbour at the end of the flood and then carry the tide to arrive at Vannes, some 11 miles away, at the top of the tide. Concerned about his draught this had been Hans' plan and his meticulous calculations had shown he would arrive with a little under half a metre to spare. He had, though, overestimated the benefit he would get from the tide so by the time he arrived at Vannes the ebb had started to run. He had also reckoned without the firmly established high pressure and strong north easterlies that had been blowing for several days.

Still, he thought, as *Matilde* edged slowly along the tree-lined canal and nosed her bows past the gates, there should be plenty to spare. Under the wary gaze of the lock keeper she eased ahead and just as Hans started to breathe a sigh of relief there was a solid scraping and grating noise and *Matilde* came to a sudden stop, with the heel of her keel, her maximum draught, firmly grounded on the lock's concrete sill. A burst ahead with the engine, more grating and still she stuck, if anything more firmly, right between the lock gates and so preventing them from closing. With visions of being besieged by hordes of angry Frenchmen as the basin drained on the ebb, he gave her full throttle ahead but again to no avail. Urgent and drastic action was needed, but what?   AB

———————

Whatever Hans does he is going to have to do it fast. Every minute of delay just makes his problem worse.

He has three options. Run out a warp to a strong point in the marina ahead or to a tree on the other side of the canal astern and use the windlass to haul her off, shift weight forward to reduce the draught aft, or heel her over by taking the spinnaker halyard to a strong point on the side of the lock and heaving on the windlass, again with the aim of reducing the draft.

What Hans can only guess at is whether he is aground on the top of the sill or if he is perched on the edge of it. After his burst of power ahead I would expect that he is probably sitting right on top of it.

The direct haul ahead or astern depends on either a very long throw with a heaving line (and someone to catch it and haul across and secure a warp) or a boat to run the warp out. Neither are likely to be instantly available, so I think he should discard that option.

Trimming by the head is attractive because it depends only on his own resources. The question is, can he move enough weight, quickly enough for it to be effective? In a boat of this size I would suspect that moving a 200lb man from stern to stem will increase the freeboard at the stern by about an inch. The deepest part of the keel is likely to be about half way between the stern and the mid-point of the boat so the man moved from right aft to right forward is going to produce an effective reduction in draft of half an inch. How many 200lb men did he have sitting on the taffrail when he grounded or how many portable but heavy items of gear are there at the back of the boat ready to be carried to the bows? Hans is probably going to need to lift the heel by several inches and I doubt if he is going to find enough portable weight to achieve that in time.

The heeling option remains. The lock keeper is close at hand and it shouldn't be too difficult to get the end of the spinnaker halyard ashore to him. He has probably played this game before so even with a language barrier to overcome there should not be too much difficulty explaining what is required of him by way of attaching the end of the halyard to a strong point, as far as possible from the lock wall. A head rope is also going to be needed, to the other side of the lock, so that the pull on the halyard does not simply cause the boat to pivot on her heel. Then it is just a question of hauling on the end of the halyard, if necessary tailing it onto the windlass to achieve enough power. With the boat heeled 15 degrees the draft will be reduced about $2\frac{1}{2}$ inches, at 25 degrees it will be reduced by 7 inche . The trick will be to keep the engine driving ahead so that as she starts to lift she will move ahead and not sideways.

Hopefully Hans had worked all this out as part of a contingency plan, well in advance. If not, his only hope of surviving a wave of Gallic fury lies in a large crew of Dutchmen, all possessed of an ample measure of the national talent for Dyke plugging.   BA

––––––––

I could only improve on Bill's suggestions in one way. Before taking any other action Hans could try one immediate ploy: to go hard astern back to where he knows there is deeper water. He might be just on the edge of the sill and be able to get her off backwards. Even though the engine will probably develop less thrust astern than ahead, if he sends all crew forward at the same time it might succeed and need only take a couple of minutes. If it fails then it's time to follow Bill's advice. And it should work. I have to confess to being the navigator on board a yacht in exactly this situation and this location. We managed to get off using brute force. All crew went forward and with full throttle we bumped and ground our way ahead over the sill into deep water the other side. Although we didn't exactly receive a round of applause, it was a very relieved lock keeper who watched us leave a couple of days later – this time without touching.   AB

Groan you may, but go you must

'Thank goodness for that!' muttered Philip as he brought his 36ft heavy displacement cruising ketch, the *Guernsey Cow*, around the last corner and up to the quay at Poole, a harbour on the south coast of England. The light was fading and it was August National Holiday. Maud had somehow managed to put the two kids to bed as they came up the long harbour and it looked as though they were in for a quiet night.

He was tired after the 15-hour passage from France and he knew that Maud was too. She'd been sick most of the way and looked worn out now.

The whole quay as far up as the bridge was full of boats rafted three and four deep and no-one looked anxious to have *Guernsey Cow* alongside. The only place left was at the seaward end of the wall, next to a 28ft racing yacht lying alone astern of the last raft, with no sign of anyone aboard. The berth wouldn't be sheltered in a southwesterly but the forecast seemed reasonable enough after the passage of a cold front that morning, so Philip gratefully tied up to the smaller boat, rigged shorelines and called it a day.

After the Customs had called, he and Maud wolfed a Chinese meal, drank a bottle of duty free wine and then turned in. At midnight their neighbours returned, banged about for a while, then they too went to bed. Philip put his head out of the hatch to make sure that all was well and noted that the stars were blurring out and that the moon was sporting a bright halo. He tapped the barometer and it dipped a point or so.

'Looks like a warm front again,' he said to himself. 'Still, it probably won't be here till morning, and even then it may not amount to anything. We'll be OK tonight.'

But they weren't.

Philip had been sound asleep for three hours when Maud shook him awake. She didn't need to brief him about the situation. Philip's distant warm front had turned into a vicious secondary depression. The rain was thudding onto the deck and the *Guernsey Cow* was surging and leaping about. From the seaward side came the sound of waves breaking against the topsides and from the direction of the other boat the grinding of fenders and the hollow tread of feet preceeded the now inevitable knock on the coachroof.

Maud slid back the hatch as Philip struggled into his foul weather gear.

'You'll have to clear out, Mate!' came the strident voice of the neighbouring skipper. 'We're being nipped in here. The boat's crying like a baby and the bulkheads'll start popping any minute!'

Philip glanced at his watch. There was still an hour to go before High Water. 'OK,' he said coming up on deck. There was a full gale blowing and a two foot sea was slamming into the boats. The racket of masts and rigging was terrific. *Guernsey Cow* must have outweighed her neighbour by three to one, and even if she hadn't, this berth was no place to be. She had to get off, but how?

Philip started up the engine and Maud pushed off up forward, helped by three strapping lads from the racing yacht. But they might as well have pushed a brick wall. There was a 'bang' as a fender between the two boats burst, followed by the sound of splintering fibreglass as *Guernsey Cow* began to hammer at the little boat's toe rail.

'What the hell do we do now?' asked Philip desperately.

Fortunately, the skipper of the racing boat had several useful ideas. . . .   TC

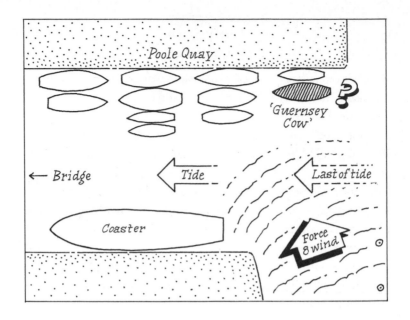

Poole Quay has bred more pyjama panics than a French farce. About all Philip has going for him is that last bit of flood tide. It looks as if easing Guernsey Cow's *stern line and back spring would (with a bit of hardening in forward) allow a gap to open between the sterns which the current acting on a heavy and long keeled hull would soon widen. Then its' let go all and full astern with all she's got. After that she'd either have to be taken out and anchored or try for a temporary berth alongside the coaster. 'Sorry mate yer can't lie 'ere.'* JDS

———

I'd go along with Des, though a helping of rudder to port might be useful to assist the tide. If this doesn't work *Guernsey Cow* will have to spring off. She'll do this by letting go all her lines except the bow spring and motoring ahead against it with her rudder to starboard, and lots of fenders around her starboard bow. That will do the trick of getting her stern well out. She can then let go and power out astern to go seeking pastures new. TC

Catastrophe

Julian Mason had never sailed a catamaran before. It was with some trepidation that he accepted Phil Oakley's invitation race one. Julian was flattered to be invited, because Phil and his crew had something of a reputation as hot-shot racers. He might have felt rather differently had he known that four others had already turned down the invitation.

Phil's cat had no pretentions to comfort. She was built ten years ago for racing, the accommodation was minimal and the rig seemed complicated and, to Julian who was used to conventional cruising boats, much too powerful for the slender hulls to support.

The race was the club end of season jolly across to France, start on Friday night, dinner ashore on Saturday and sail for home in the early hours of Sunday morning. Phil decided that they should sail in two watches, he would take one with Julian and the other two members of the crew, who knew the boat well, would take the other.

During the race Julian began to understand the unusual features of the rig. The powerful 8:1 mainsheet was used like a kicking strap to take the twist out of the main and the traveller, which ran on a wide semi-circular track, was used to trim the mainsail.

They won the race, dinner was a gastronomic and social event of considerable merit and they sailed at 0200 on Sunday morning filled with a spirit on confidence.

Phil and Julian took the first watch. It was a clear night with almost perfect sailing conditions, 15 knots of wind from the port quarter and, with the boat doing 9 knots, that put the apparent wind dead on the port beam.

For the first half hour of the watch Phil was chatting enthusiastically, about the dinner, the race and sailing in general. Then he started to go quiet. Even in the dim glow of the compass light Julian could see that the colour had drained from his face.

Phil asked Julian to take the helm. 'Feels like oysters' revenge, drat it' he mumbled as he made for the hatch. 'You should be OK on your own for a while, no need to wake the others.'

At first Julian felt apprehensive about being alone in the cockpit, but after a few minutes he began to enjoy the exhilaration of racing northward through the night, with the speed indicator needle hovering close to 10 knots. The boat had been designed for single-handed sailing, the sheets and traveller were all on jamming cleats close to hand, so if anything unexpected did happen there should be no problem about manoeuvring quickly.

Julian was so preoccupied with the detail of the boat and the speed that he didn't notice the dark cloud spreading across the horizon to windward. As the squall struck time seem to go into slow motion, he was aware of the wind indicator reading 30 knots, of the weather hull starting to lift out of the water and of the lee bow disappearing into a plume of erie green spray.

Should he bear away or luff? Dump the mainsheet, the traveller or the genoa sheet?

He had only seconds in which to do *something* to avoid a catastrophe. What should he do? BA

I've only once sailed in a fast multi and I scared both myself and the owner. In this case (knowing nothing of such behemoths) I would let fly the genoa to avert capsize and further slow her by easing the mainsheet to reduce drive, then bear off on a near-run. With no following sea she shouldn't drive under. JDS

The answer given by Des is almost exactly right, but I would suggest the following rather fuller explanation.

The important thing is NOT to luff and NOT to ease the mainsheet. Bear away onto a dead run, let go the jib sheet and perhaps ease the traveller to reduce the risk of an accidental gybe. It is likely that the rest of the crew will be on deck before you have time to call them but if the after-effects of the party have dulled their sense of self-preservation, shout for them to come on deck. You will certainly need them to help shorten sail and the sight of the skipper struggling through the hatch with his trousers round his ankles should add some much-needed comic relief to a very tense situation.

The answer would be a little different if the main had a conventional kicking strap but without one easing the mainsheet tends to allow too much twist in the sail, pushing the bow down and causing a pitch-pole. Luffing will almost certainly cause a capsize, turning down wind in a very fast boat reduces the relative wind, which is exactly what you want to achieve.   BA

The crunch

Cruncher of Cowes is a 30ft modern cruising sloop. She has a roller headsail, a slab-reefing mainsail and she performs well. She has a crew of three. Jasper, the skipper, is elderly, a trifle impulsive, and is delighted with the performance of his latest boat. He is discovering that he can enjoy manoeuvres with her which his previous more pedestrian vessels did not encourage him to attempt. His daughter, Tamsin, is a highly competent yachtswoman, having sailed with her Dad since she could walk, and Charles, her husband, is a rugby flank forward enjoying a summer break from murdering fly-halves. Charles' only sailing experience is with the other two and he is generally rated for muscular capacity rather than seamanship.

On the day in question the *Cruncher* is anchored in Studland Bay, a popular open roadstead on the South Coast of England. The anchorage is crowded but there is a little space astern of her. The tide, which doesn't greatly affect the boats in the bay, has just turned fair in the offing. Jasper and Co have been waiting for this and are now ready to get under way.

They look to windward to where they estimate their anchor is set. On one side of the anchor at a distance of about four boats' lengths an old gaffer with a long bowsprit is lying quietly to her heavy chain cable. Her skipper is sitting in her cockpit enjoying a cup of something while his dog stares challengingly at them. Jasper has been nostalgically admiring this craft. He always anchors on chain himself, even in his new lightweight flyer.

On their other bow, lying a little further back than the old gaffer, is a catamaran, apparently untended. She is anchored on nylon rope and is sailing around from left to right in the force 4 breeze. At one end of her surging progress she is within a couple of lengths of *Cruncher*'s anchor, while at the other end she is 50yds away. Her gyration period takes about a minute, but does not appear to be entirely predictable.

Charles glances astern. There is a reasonable gap of 40 or 50 yards before the next group of boats and, ranged out on either side of them is an assortment of vessels allowing various possible paths of exit, but he doesn't like the look of the old gaffer and the catamaran.

'Shall I get the engine going, Dad?' he offers.

'Can't see the need for that,' replies Jasper. 'We'll just hoist the main, pull her up to the anchor, unroll some jib, and break out the hook when the cat's furthest away from us; then we'll back the jib and sail off closehauled round the cat's bows.'

That sounds logical enough to Charles, who always admires the old man's positive approach. So he throws off the sail ties and hoists away.

But Tamsin is looking doubtful. 'Do you think this is wise, Dad?' she queries as the main begins to flog. 'I'm not convinced that . . .' The thundering sail drowns her voice. 'So why,' she is now continuing, 'don't we . . . instead?'

Jasper thinks for a moment, then nods in agreement. Five minutes later *Cruncher of Cowes* is sailing away smoothly on the first of the tide. What was Tamsin concerned about, and what other useful suggestions could she have been making to Jasper?   TC

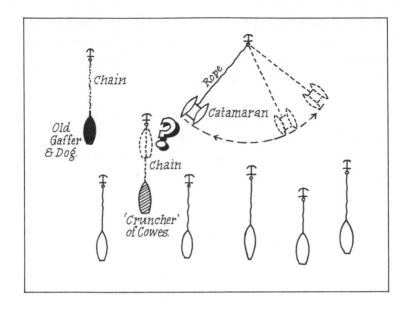

There are two snags with Jasper's plan. First, he cannot know the exact position of his anchor in relation to the two boats ahead. Secondly he cannot be sure that the anchor will break out exactly when he wants it to, it may start to come home a little earlier than he anticipates, it may hold a little longer than he would wish. Add to these the acknowledged unpredictability of the catamaran's gyrations and we have, as Tamsin has obviously realised, a thoroughly dodgy manoeuvre in which the most important element is luck.

The thoroughly dull answer would be to start the motor so that it is available to give a kick ahead or astern at the vital moment. It may not be needed but it could save an embarrassingly close encounter. On the other hand it would ruin the satisfaction of leaving the anchorage under sail even to have the beast at immediate readiness.

A safer way to leave the berth would be to drop astern. Accomplishing this is going to call for restraint, particularly from Charles who could no doubt heave in the cable fast enough to have the boat up to planing speed before the anchor broke out (or snagged and snubbed so hard that it pulled the stemhead under water.) Dropping astern out of an anchor berth calls *for patience and a very slow recovery of the anchor cable. As soon as the anchor starts to drag a slight sternboard can be encouraged by pushing the boom out to windward and the headsail can be sheeted to weather as it is unrolled.*

A safe but very tedious option would be to recover half the cable and then let go the kedge, so that you have a positive means of pulling back out of the gap between the gaffer and the cat — but why go to all that trouble when you could solve the problem with a quick burst on the engine. BA

I concur with Bill's analysis of that situation. If I were Jasper, I'd go for the 'gentle stern-board' solution which I'm sure Tamsin has been suggesting. The problem attached to such a manoeuvre is that unless the mainsheet is eased fully, the boat may refuse to bear away quickly enough to clear the anchored vessels on either side of her as she sails out. If the boom is pushed out in order to 'reverse' away from the point where the anchor is weighed this problem will not arise because the sheet is already overhauled.

It would be a shame to start the engine, especially as Jasper is such a sportsman. TC

A prudent navigator

Tony looked up from the chart table, aware that Edward was peering over his shoulder at the chart.

'What are you doing?' Edward asked. 'The next leg across the estuary should be straight forward. The distance is 25 miles, we're doing five knots. The tide will be flooding for the next two hours, slack for an hour and then ebbing for two hours. All you have to do is lay off a course and steer it, the tidal streams will cancel each other out. Why are you making such a meal of it? The flood will be running at two knots for an hour, then at one knot for the next hour, but you don't have to plot all that because it will be cancelled out during the last two hours of the passage by the ebb.'

'It isn't as simple as that.' Tony answered.

The passage which they were discussing is shown on the sketch chart. They were approaching point A, on the south side of the estuary and making for point B on the north side. Edward's summary of the distance, speed and tidal streams were correct. Was he also correct in his succinct statement of the simple navigational plan?   BA

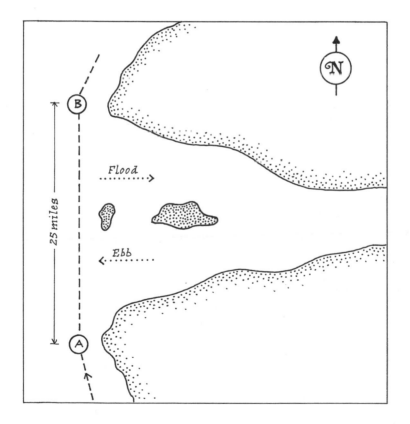

Tony is quite right. Edward should immediately return to his duties (cleaning the heads, perhaps?) and let Tony concentrate on organising the shortest safe passage between A and B.

Edward's problem stems from having failed to attend a particular lesson on his night-school course last winter. He went to the one where the question of making a passage across a tidal stream expected to turn was discussed, but he missed the following week.

Had there been no shoals in the mouth of the estuary Edward's suggestion to Tony would have been in order. To make the passage without laying off for the tide could have saved them a substantial amount of distance to be run. The boat would have been set three miles inshore of the rhumb line by the flood, then set three miles back again by the ebb, conveniently rejoining the rhumb-line at point B (illustration 1). They

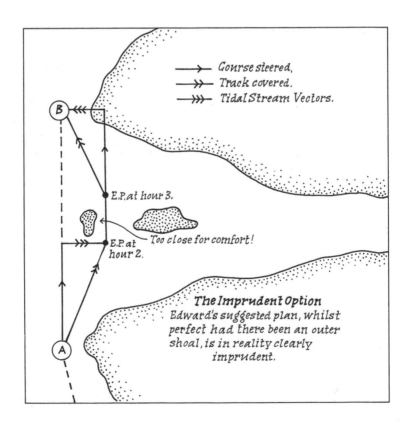

Course steered.
Track covered.
Tidal Stream Vectors.

E.P. at hour 3.

Too close for comfort!

E.P. at hour 2.

The Imprudent Option
Edward's suggested plan, whilst perfect had there been an outer shoal, is in reality clearly imprudent.

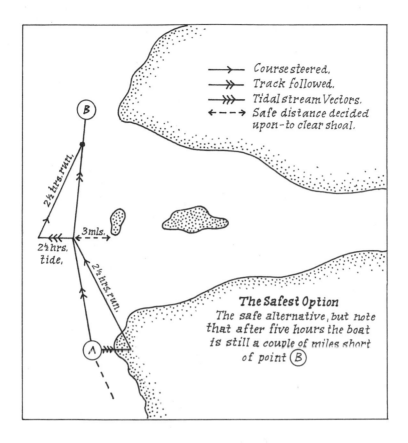

Course steered.
Track followed.
Tidal stream Vectors.
Safe distance decided
upon - to clear shoal.

2½ hrs. run.

2½ hrs. tide.

3 mls.

2½ hrs. run.

B

A

The Safest Option
The safe alternative, but note
that after five hours the boat
is still a couple of miles short
of point (B)

would have travelled further over the ground, but by steering straight for their destination their distance to run through the water would be the minimum possible. In other words, all the extra ground they covered would be supplied 'free' by the tidal stream.

If, however, they had laid off a new course for each hour of tide in order to stay on the rhumb line, they would have involved themselves in needless course alterations and needless extra distance to run.

This much Edward has learned.

What he has not thought out is that if they adhere to his policy on this occasion the first two hours of tide are going to set the yacht perilously close to the outer shoal. It is possible in theory that the full three-mile set predicted will leave them inshore of this horror, but it would be an

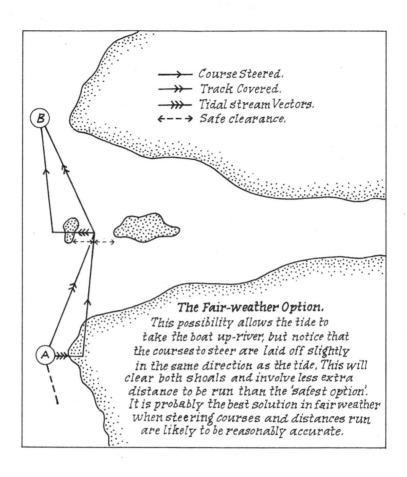

Course Steered.
Track Covered.
Tidal stream Vectors.
Safe clearance.

The Fair-weather Option.
This possibility allows the tide to
take the boat up-river, but notice that
the courses to steer are laid off slightly
in the same direction as the tide. This will
clear both shoals and involve less extra
distance to be run than the 'safest option'.
It is probably the best solution in fair weather
when steering courses and distances run
are likely to be reasonably accurate.

imprudent navigator who relied upon tidal stream predictions and the accuracy of his own log and compass so slavishly. In practice the predictions rarely prove perfectly accurate on the day and the helmsman who can be relied upon to steer a perfect course is a rare bird indeed. Stranding would be nothing less than Edward's just desserts.

What Tony is considering is whether to lay off enough in the first two hours to take him well to seaward of the outer shoal (illustration 2) and then work back to point B accordingly, or whether to allow the tide to set him in but actually to steer a touch to port of the rhumb line in order to be certain of being set inshore of the outer obstruction (illustration 3). The inner shoal will then become of interest to him but since he will be passing *between the two at slack water he may well feel that his Estimated Position after two hours will be adequate to steer safely through this five-mile passage. It is a pity that there are absolutely no marks of any kind on which Tony could confirm his position, but there are not, so he is left entirely to the mercies of log, compass and tidal predictions.*

If the weather is fair he will probably opt for the latter course of action, which will certainly involve him in less extra distance to sail. If conditions are poor, however, or he is less than totally sure of his instruments, he will play absolutely safe and opt for the longer, outside passage.

Once Tony's decision has been made, he can go on deck to enjoy the yachting, and invite Edward to brew the tea.   TC

The tidal streams will definitely cancel out over the passage but it would certainly be imprudent simply to accept that and steer the bearing from departure point to destination. In the middle of the passage the yacht will be three miles off the direct line and the navigator needs to plot that to make sure that she will not be in any danger. Tom's solutions need no further comment from me.   BA

Heavy lift

The boat was laid up afloat, the mast out of her and not much in way of gear left aboard her but her owner felt sure that a couple of people would be able to raise the modest little engine off the beds by hand, he only wanted to get a couple of short baulks under it so that he could replace the sump tray. Had he been able to get alongside a quay with a crane it would of course have been no bother at all.

The two of them soon found that the engine was heavier than it looked, moreover there wasn't room for the two men both to get a good grip on it and so they cast around for the means to rig a simple tackle. They found a suitable length of rope and a couple of single sheave blocks, double-becketed, but was that much of an advantage? They found a stout enough short spar to lay across the top of the companionway from which the tackle could be suspended and they then rigged up a single purchase or gun tackle, this only gave them a power of 2:1 however because the upper block was fixed and the pull on the fall was downwards.

After a bit of thought they reversed it so that the pull was upwards from the lower block which was attached to the engine; this gave them a power of 3:1 and it was almost, but not quite, sufficient. If only we had a double and a single block we'd be laughing they said. Then the owner had an idea. He made yet another arrangement of the two single sheave blocks and this time they had a power of 4:1, what did they do?   JDS

––––––––––

Noah had exactly the same problem when he was unloading the ark, so I can do no better than recount his solution.

The hold of the ark had two decks, the upper served by a door in the side. Noah was a tidy-minded man, he stowed the animals in the A–M category, which included the heavy ones such as the Bison, the Camel, the Horse and the Elephant on the upper of the two decks. After grounding, these beasts simply walked down the gang-plank onto the land.

The animals on the lower deck, the N–Z group, had to be hoisted out. This was no problem, until it came to the Zebras. Finding two double-becketed blocks, a short stout spar and a length of rope to hand, Mr and Mrs Noah managed, after quite a struggle, to hoist the Zebra mare to the level of the upper hold with the blocks rigged to advantage giving a 3:1 power ratio.

The Zebra stallion, however, was an altogether larger beast and they knew that they were going to need more mechanical advantage if they were going to shift him.

'We need a double sheave' said Mrs Noah. 'Then we could add another moving part. Every time you add another moving part you increase the

mechanical advantage. Without another sheave in the system we can't get from the third to the fourth level of power.'

Mr Noah, as well as being a mean hand with the adze and an inspired amateur meteorologist, knew a thing or two about basic mechanics.

'We must take a different approach' he said. 'By adding sheaves you add to the power. If we could rig our two blocks in tandem, with one pulling from the hauling end of the other, we could multiply the power. Yes, that's it, by adding the sheaves together we can only go to the third level of power, to go to the fourth we must multiply.'

He rigged his two blocks as shown in the diagram, it worked, but his words of wisdom have been mis-quoted ever since.　　　　　BA

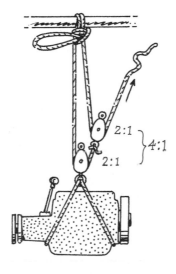

Yes. What they rigged was an inverted whip-on-whip. One block was secured to the engine, the rope was secured to the spar above and rove through the block to give an upward pull, which by itself constituted a 2:1 power. The second block was then secured to this hauling part and similarly rove off using the other end of the rope. This arrangement has a short length of travel but they only needed a small lift. Bill Anderson is quite correct if his biblical interpretation seems a little suspect!　　　　　JDS

Disappearing shelter

In the shallow seas where the great banks spread far out to sea, a world of shoal and spitway, drying sands and winding low tide channels there can be found temporary havens where from mid-ebb to the following mid-flood sheltered lagoons appear in which a small ship may anchor for a few quiet hours. It was in one such between-tide anchorages that the yacht lay peacefully to her anchor, with her 1.5m draft she lay in 3m of water while beyond the banks the wind was freshening and the sigh of breaking water was becoming audible.

They had entered via a narrow gut when the rest of the banks were still awash on the ebb, an easy entrance guided by a small buoy to port and the echo sounder and the intention had been to stay in the anchorage until the next flood was fully made, because conditions had been quite calm then. Now though things have altered and prudence dictates that they leave as soon as possible. There is a range of 3.6m that day and by half-flood the shelter will have disappeared. The time is low water and dusk is at hand, the small buoy will be invisible soon, but with the chart showing 0.3m in the channel they will have to leave no earlier than half-flood because there will be a sea running.

They calculate that by half flood the range will have made 1.80m which added to the 0.3m in the entrance gives them 2.1m depth, which with their draft of 1.5m leaves only 0.60m under their keel — barely enough if a sea is breaking.

Their biggest problem though will be to find the entrance in the dark. There are no buoy lights within range to provide an accurate fix and following the steep-to edge of the bank while beam-on to wind and by then breaking wave would be feasable only in theory. How did they go about it?   JDS

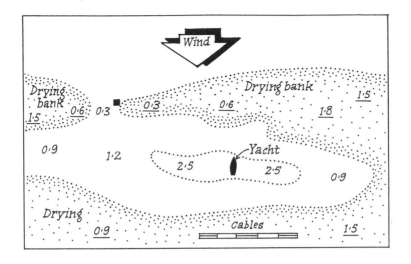

They made a brave try but they knew that the odds on it working were no better than 50–50. Luck was not on their side and the boat was hammered to fragments on the sands, but at least they did make the best possible attempt to extricate themselves from a very tricky situation.

They thought about waiting for high water when they would, at least in theory, have a very wide gap with a depth of over two metres to aim for. They decided against it, however, as both wind and sea were rising and any delay was only going to make things worse.

They used the last of the light, while they could still see the buoy, to shift berth as close to the buoy as possible. This meant that when the time came to try to escape they were only 2½ cables from the entrance instead of six. By halving the distance they doubled the acceptable margin of error. They also took great care to get an accurate bearing of the buoy as they let go in the new anchor berth.

At half-tide they started the engine, weighed anchor and headed off at full power along the bearing of the buoy. They allowed nothing for leeway as they needed to be set to port to avoid clipping the sand bank on the eastern side of the entrance.

The log showed that they were making 5 knots, so it was a 6-minute run to the entrance. After 3 minutes they switched on their most powerful torch to search for the buoy. After 6½ minutes the log showed a distance run of 0.25 miles, the echo sounder was reading just over two metres and they still hadn't seen the buoy. They turned north. Seconds later they spotted the buoy on the starboard bow, rather broader than they had hoped. As they turned to starboard the keel hit the sand and almost simultaneously they were overwhelmed by a foaming breaker.

They took to the liferaft and survived but the yacht was a total loss.

The escape plan was the best one possible but to succeed the navigation must be more accurate than plus or minus 50 yards. In heavy weather, getting under weigh and gathering way it is impossible to guarantee that level of precision. It might have worked but . . .   BA

———————

Let's not be pessimistic. To begin with they will have better than 2.1 m in the channel when they attempt to leave, they will have more like 2.6m because the low water this day is not falling to chart datum by 0.5m, at low tide they found a depth of 3m in a position shown on the chart to have 2.5m.

With a draft of 1.5m this bonus means that in a short while they will be able to get their anchor and while there is still some daylight left begin feeling their way towards the still visible entrance, anchoring again on a short scope as close to it as they can manage, perhaps within little more than a cable's length of it. From here a very careful safe line bearing is taken on the buoy and a course is plotted. The yacht is likely to lie quietly at anchor facing the entrance, all they must do is wait and monitor the rising depth. Bill Anderson doesn't seem to have spotted that there is 0.5m more water at LW than the chart shows and that they could have got closer to the entrance while waiting for the tide to rise, but it's debatable.   JDS

PART THREE

Suddenly there is an almighty crash from up for'd . . .

Quick thinking

We all dread what is perhaps the worst possible situation at sea: being holed and having to abandon ship in a hurry.

Imagine you are on passage from Lowestoft to Bergen in mid June. You are out of the shipping lanes but there are fishing fleets in the vicinity. You are almost exactly half way on the passage so out of range of any Coast Radio stations. Your boat is a modern grp sloop and well equipped for such a passage – equipment includes a 4-man liferaft and you have four on board. The yacht is also equipped with VHF radio and all normal safety gear but before you left you did not have the foresight to pack a panic bag. The wind is force 4, the sea calm and visibility good though no lights are in sight. It is 0300, two crew are asleep below decks, two of you are on watch.

Suddenly there is an almighty crash from for'd and seconds later you see the protruding corner of a semi-submerged container floating past. You go below to find water rushing in through a gaping hole in the forecabin below the waterline. There is obviously no way that you can stem the flood and your first priority is to abandon ship. You probably have five minutes before the yacht sinks.

In one minute write down two lists. The first is your list of immediate actions to take, including instructions to the crew who are now all awake. The second list is of items of equipment you will take with you in the liferaft to help survival. Starting from Now . . .   AB

Actions to take
- *Turn out watch below*
- *Issue Mayday on VHF*
- *Fire first red rocket flare*
- *Launch liferaft*

- *Issue life-jackets*
- *Assemble panic gear*
- *Stay with yacht until last possible moment in order to issue more Maydays and gather as much gear as possible for the raft*
- *Activate EPIRB (Emergency position indicating radio beacon)*

Panic Items
Water
Food/tin opener/spoon
Clothes
Flares
Bucket
EPIRB
Log Book
First Aid Kit
Knife
Rope
String
Torch
Shakespeare/Bible   TC

You have, in fact, got more than one minute. Even with a large hole in the hull, although the initial inrush of water will be very rapid, as the boat settles so it will slow. Even so, in the evitable chaos and, perhaps, panic a minute may be the most thinking time the skipper will have. It is also likely to be the most taxing period in his sailing life and it will have paid him, before a passage of this duration, to have thought through the possibility, prepared a 'panic bag' with essentials and briefed his crew. He has three priorities and it is vital that they are dealt with in order. These are: survival, rescue and comfort/convenience.

Whilst I don't disagree with any of Tom's suggestions and the order in which he has placed them, he has missed one element. The issuing of crew orders in view of their various abilities. It might be:

'John and Mary, launch the liferaft then fire two parachute flares a minute apart. Margaret, take that sleeping bag and stuff it with the spare water carrier, some food, the flares, EPIRB and as many clothes as you can fit in.' He should himself remain in the 'command' position, operating the VHF before the rising water kills the batteries and issuing instructions. Paniky crew should be given simple but not vital jobs. It should be he too who gives the order to abandon ship and the sequence for boarding the liferaft — remembering the advice not to take to the raft until you have to step up onto it but not leaving things so late as to have to swim for it.

The only items of gear I would add are life harnesses and basic navigational gear, even if just the chart and a hand bearing compass. If the crew do find themselves in the water they stand a far better chance of survival if clipped together whilst if they are drifting for any length of time a rough position check might help them to decide when to use their precious flares as they pass near rigs or shipping lanes.   AB

Dawn manoeuvres

It was one of those grey, misty summer dawns when there is no clear definition between day and night, no sun to greet and warm night watch weary yachtsmen. We were on passage from Lymington to L'Aberwrac'h and were approaching the north east corner of the central Channel separation scheme, some 20 miles south of Portland Bill. Shipping had been sparse though the lights of a few vessels had been identified heading towards the west going TSS. All was in order, the northwesterly force 4 giving us an unexpectedly fast passage so far.

Our only concern at the minute, apart from the doorstep ham and egg sandwich that John was preparing in the galley, were the gyrations of a set of as yet unidentified lights on the starboard bow. It was obviously a large vessel, though exactly what was unclear. Some red flashing lights hovering nearby we took to be helicopters and so made the assumption that it was a naval vessel on manoeuvres.

She had started on the starboard bow, steamed rapidly across until on the port bow and in the last few minutes moved back again to her present position where she lay, apparently motionless, about two miles away attended by her two red flashing dragonfly accolytes. Two miles seemed safe enough and our interest was more academic than real concern. I turned my attention to breakfast leaving John keeping a lookout.

Five minutes later he called down. 'Looks like an aircraft carrier'. I tuned the VHF to Channel 16 and went to have a look. Sure enough, in the strengthening light there she was on the horizon, her flat top and superstructure distinctive and now steaming at an oblique angle towards us, perhaps a mile distant. 'I wonder whether it's the one the Navy has just sold to India,' John mused, 'I hope they're not having driving lessons.'

As he spoke the aspect of the aircraft carrier changed until both red and green lights were clearly visible. My concern was real enough now, especially as I could plainly see the white bone in her teeth as she thundered directly towards us like a charging rhino, closing the distance perceptibly by the second.

'Right Mr Yachtmaster Offshore,' muttered John, 'what the hell are you going to do about that?' AB

A nasty situation, this one. Until the arrival of the aircraft carrier, probably the skipper's biggest problem was what he was going to do about the central Channel separation scheme. Passagemakers from the west Solent to northwest Brittany often have to make an awkward decision about that. The current business, however, has nothing to do with the Traffic Separation Scheme at all.

This is a situation in which the yacht is going to be well advised to keep clear of the ship. The question is, how? The aircraft carrier hasn't done much recently to establish confidence that she will maintain her present course and speed for very long. If the yachtmaster and his mate do what

*would otherwise be the right thing and haul their wind up to starboard,
how are they to rely on the ship not turning to port and finishing them off?*

*There are two possible answers to this, and if matters become any
graver than they already are, the yacht's crew would do well to consider
activating both of them. It seems that the ship has not seen the yacht in the
grey morning. If, however, the yachtsmen can successfully draw attention
to themselves having turned to starboard, all will be well.*

Unless, of course, the fighting ship is on a yacht-gobbling binge.

*The first and tidiest action is to call up the carrier on Channel 16. The
initial call could go something like this: 'Aircraft Carrier manoeuvring 20
miles south of Portland Bill, this is the sailing yacht* Loiterer *one mile
ahead of you.' When she comes back (if she does) and indicates a working
channel the yacht has simply to advise the warship of her presence and
indicate her course alteration. She'll need to be quick, but once radio
contact has been established, there should be no further problems.*

*If the attempt fails, and a critical stage seems to be approaching, the
second thing to do is to show the warship a white hand-held flare. It is still
dark enough for this to be highly effective. Warships generally keep a first-
class look-out and there is no doubt that the flare will be seen. The watch
officer will probably react instinctively and order a turn to starboard and
since this will fit in with the yacht's favoured course alteration, the danger
should shortly be past and gone.*

*Let's hope it doesn't come to that, though. Ignited flares are dangerous
things on board small sailing yachts and if John is asked to fire one, the
carrier's watch officer will find himself with some explaining to do to his
captain.*

*He'll have to log the white flare and the question may well be asked,
'What was the ship doing to allow the yacht to come so close?'*

*'Practising to defend the realm,' may not be accepted as a good enough
answer.* TC

I really can't add anything to Tom's suggestion. Warships on
exercise can appear to be behaving erratically for no apparent

reason — they might be sub hunting, for example, so what you are seeing on the surface is only half the story. The closest encounter I had with a warship was 10 years ago when the cruising chute made its first appearance. We were on passage from Falmouth to Poole and were closing Portland Bill and as the wind freed hoisted our new multi-coloured chute. For a while we had been able to see a couple of frigates and as we could hear clear pings through the hull assumed they were on exercise with a submarine. Suddenly one of the destroyers broke away from the other and headed towards us at high speed. She must have been doing well over 25 knots as she crossed our stern a cable distant, skidded round in a tight turn and came to a halt close to leeward. Our alarm turned to amusement when their Tannoy crackled into life. 'Ahoy there, is that one of those new cruising chutes? . . .' AB

Violet conflict

'It's quite straightforward really.' He paused for another sip of his Scotch. 'Once you're out of the harbour keep the Hinguette can buoy to starboard then shape up to leave the Demie de Passe tower a couple of cables to the north. A course of around 110 degrees will take you towards the Canger Rock beacon but before you get there you should see the Conchière Rock beacon — it's very distinctive, all bent over with a C on top. . .' He continued as my mind wandered, looking out over the packed harbour of St Helier on Jersey.

We were following the good suggestion of Mr Adlard Coles and seeking local advice in the hospitable St Helier Yacht Club. From here we planned to head for the small drying harbour of Carteret on the west coast of the French Cotentin peninsula. Our course would take us through some of the rockiest waters I had sailed and it was the skipper's intention to take the short cut around Jersey's south east corner via the Violet Channel. Whilst I had done a fair amount of dinghy sailing and a little coastal cruising this was my first cruise going foreign and I had welcomed the chance to give up a couple of weeks of my school holidays and fairly jumped at the opportunity to go along when Henry, the sailing club commodore, invited me to join the crew of *Nimbus* on a Channel Islands cruise. Henry – he insisted on christian names though I still found it awkward – was headmaster of the local school and a paternalistic and slightly daunting figure. He had, so far during this cruise, appeared to be a competent navigator. Although the chart table was strictly his territory, he didn't object to my 'doodling', as he put it, following our progress on the chart and plotting the occasional hand bearing fix.

'Top up my glass, there's a good lad.' A hand clutching a tumbler appeared in the companionway. 'And don't spend too long down there, you're missing some glorious sailing.' I refilled the glass from the stock of duty free and went on deck. It was indeed superb sailing. The light southerly breeze pushed us gently along at about 4 knots and to the north the black teeth of rocks contrasted starkly with the bright green of Jersey's fields, the sunlight occasionally reflecting off the roofs of glasshouses. Ahead and to port the Conchière beacon was clearly visible. 'See that?' He nodded in the direction of the beacon. 'We'll go on past him for a mile or so and then it'll be clear through to Carteret – though we'll need to keep a careful eye out south of the Ecrehous.' I went below again to check the chart and the pilot. His description made it sound simple. The rock peppered chart, to my inexperienced eyes, told another story.

A short while later I was aware of the *Nimbus* changing course. I idly checked the compass. We were now headed due north. I had a dry mouth as I checked the chart again. There was only one place that course would take us – straight in amongst the rocks.

'What's the matter boy?' queried Henry as I shot into the cockpit. 'Seen a ghost or something?' Although we were still in deep water I could clearly see the weed covered wicked looking rocks sliding by on both sides. And who knows what might lie ahead. If you were me, what would you do now?   AB

You can't help feeling sorry for the lad, can you? Here he is, about to be ship-wrecked by an ancient mariner who clearly ought to know better, and from all accounts usually does. Right now it looks as if the boy knows the score while Henry does not. The trouble is, Henry will be unwilling to take seriously any suggestions that are put to him. One thing is certain, our young friend must act, and act with extreme dispatch.

The first possibility, which he may discount with regret, is to creep up on Henry with a winch handle and award him 'the Star of Lewmar'. Once his skipper is unconscious, the cabin boy can immediately put the ship onto a reciprocal course away from danger and affirm later that the boom unexpectedly fell on Henry's head.

The alternatives to this neat solution involve firmness and tact of a high order. He could try the innocent question approach. 'Gosh, Henry, isn't it exciting to be yachting along watching all those jagged black rocks just under the water?' Or maybe, 'I say, Henry, do you think the echo sounder can have gone wrong? There's only 3cm under the keel and it seems to be shoaling?'

It may even be worth taking the Bull by the Horns, or the Headmaster by the Mortarboard. 'I don't want to be mutinous, or anything, Henry, but according to the chart, if we steer due North from Conchière, we'll be into the bricks in short order. I'll just pass you the chart so you can show me if I'm wrong.'

The truly devious solution is to offer to take the helm and then steer something other than the course demanded, but this could turn out to be the road to ruin. Honesty or violence seem to be the only viable answers.

Good luck, boy. You're going to need it. I only hope that Henry is the sort of skipper who will have been mellowed by his lunchtime dram. When I was your age, they all seemed to turn fighting mad. . . .   TC

Perhaps a question of psychology might have been more appropriate for this one. However, although it is not strictly about seamanship, psychology is an important part of the smooth running of a yacht at sea both in terms of the way the skipper handles his crew and the way they, in turn, react to him.

Henry is at fault on several counts, not least of all in allowing the fine weather and his lunchtime dram to let his navigation in these tricky waters slip. He would probably be more at home on a sail training vessel than on his own boat with a teenager as crew and unconsciously, even though outwardly relaxed and friendly, is still the headmaster at heart which leaves the lad with a severe lack of confidence. He's the one who is going to have to use psychology and tact to escape his predicament. I would suggest he could try one of two approaches. The first would be to peer over the side and comment innocently on how clear the water is because those rocks look just a few feet away. The second, with equal innocence, would be to look pointedly at the compass and then say 'oh, we're going to the north of the Ecrehous, are we'. Henry's reaction might be 'stupid boy' to either, but unless he's totally legless by now he'd be very thick skinned indeed if he didn't check out either himself and implement an immediate about turn to back track on his course.   AB

A tricky delivery

Paul is a yacht delivery skipper. For many years he has sailed and motored all sorts of yachts; ugly and beautiful, cheap and expensive, good-mannered and bad. On this occasion he is delivering a long-keeled 36ft sloop, *The Crimson Rambler*. The owner is aboard, but is not an experienced seaman, so Paul has brought along his girl-friend as a third hand. Josie is a useful watch-keeper and is extremely petite; physical strength is not her forte.

They have made a fair passage, under sail all the way and as they approach their goal, Paul realises that he is starting the engine for only the second time since their departure, apart from a two-hour session each morning, out of gear, to charge the batteries. He knows nothing about the likely characteristics of the boat under power, other than the fact that her engine is generous for her tonnage, and that the installation appears to be first class.

Paul calls up the marina for which *The Crimson Rambler* is bound and advises the dockmaster of their ETA. The dockmaster promises to meet them at the outside pontoon and direct them to a berth. The tide is flooding hard as they arrive off the marina and Paul has to round up and stem it while he talks to the dockmaster.

'Where do you want us?' he calls.

'E15,' replies the man, 'go in the next gap and you'll find it halfway down on your port side — just past that black cutter with the bowsprit sticking out.' Then he adds as an afterthought, 'I'm afraid it's down-tide!'

Paul motors around, still outside in the river and, as he orders up warps and fenders, he sizes up the situation. There are about four boats' lengths between the boats on his row of finger berths and those on the next jetty up-tide. All the berths are well equipped with solid-looking cleats, and apart from that cutter, none of the other boats are standing more than 8ft or so proud of their own pontoons.

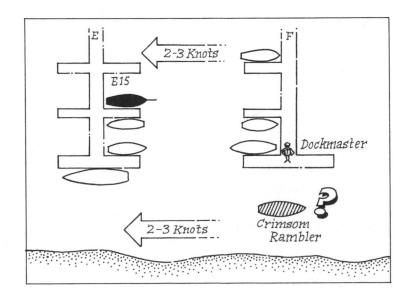

He estimates the length of E15 to be a little over 25ft. The tide seems to be running at 2 to 3 knots and there is no wind to speak of.

Bearing in mind his complement and what he does and does not know about the boat, what steps would you expect him to take to enter the berth without having *The Crimson Rambler* smashed by the pontoon, or the cutter's bowsprit, or both? TC

In theory at least and having practised out in the river Philip might position Crimson Rambler *just up-tide of her berth and stemming the current, then by decreasing revs he might be able to drop her astern under good control, might. A safer albeit inglorious alternative would be to stick her into the vacant berth in the next row up-tide, make fast a 40-metre warp (or make up one from bits and pieces) then drop her down-tide into E15.* JDS

I agree with Des. Which of his solutions is chosen on the day will depend upon Paul's character.

There is, however, a remote possibility of entering the berth going ahead, which will involve ascertaining out in the river whether the boat has a right-hand or left-hand propeller. If it is a left-hand prop, she will lay her stern over to starboard as she is put astern. This feature would enable Paul to slow her down by going astern as he makes his final turn into the berth from the vicinity of the uptide pontoons. Using the propeller, Paul might feel confident enough to go into the berth ahead, then put the engine astern and propwalk onto the finger-jetty as the owner steps ashore with a line made fast amidships to whip a turn around the first cleat on the pontoon and check the *Rambler's* way. He will have about six feet in which to progressively bring her to a halt. Since the rope is attached aboard near her pivot point, the boat will now slew round as the owner loads it up.

There is just room to attempt this manoeuvre if Paul feels the owner is up to it, but if the *Crimson Rambler* turns out to have a right-hand propeller, then pity help them. They'll be caught amidships by the black cutter, and her owner is likely to appeal very loudly indeed. On balance, I'd go for one of Des's solutions. Wouldn't you?   TC

First time foreign

The Andrews children burbled excitedly to each other. Sailing down the Lymington River was nothing new to them but this was not an ordinary weekend to Poole, Cowes or Chichester. This time they were foreign bound, for Cherbourg.

Clear of the river Dick Andrews hardened in the genoa sheet. His wife Diana was on the tiller. She was the only one of the four to whom a Channel crossing was not new. As a child she had spent many summer holidays in the Channel Islands and on the Brittany coast in her parents boat. Dick was actually the more experienced sailor, having been a keen dinghy racer but he had only started to cruise when they bought their Westerly Griffon last year so that they could take the boys sailing.

Out in the middle of the Solent Dick realised that there was more wind than he had expected. By the time he had changed down from the genoa to the working jib and tucked a slab in the main the strengthening ebb had carried them down to Hurst Narrows.

The sea in the Needles Channel was short and steep, the worst possible length for the boat and progress was slow and wet. The children became less chirpy and by the time the Needles was abeam they were silent and sodden, huddled at the front of the cockpit. Young Harry announced that he was going to be sick, and promptly proved the truth of his prophesy by vomitting over his brother.

Dick took the tiller while Diana did a cleaning job on the boys. Her attempts to persuade them to go below and get warm were firmly resisted, they were both feeling lousy and were convinced that going into the cabin would only add to their misery. Diana didn't insist, she wasn't feeling too good herself after her cleaning session.

Diana took over the tiller again and Dick went down to the chart table to plot a departure fix and lay off a course. When he appeared in the cockpit again ten minutes later he was looking as pale as his sons.

Diana laughed. 'My three tough men don't look too happy and you, Dick, look the worst of the lot.' She said. 'Take the tiller will you while I go and get us all a hot drink and a biscuit.'

Dick was reluctant. 'Are you sure this is wise?' he asked. 'We can only just lay the course for Cherbourg, at our present speed it's going to take at least 14 hours so we won't be there until midnight. And if the wind backs it will be even longer.'

'Don't be defeatist darling.' Diana answered. 'We've done the worst part, down the Needles Channel with the wind against tide is always worse than out in the open sea. In any case the ebb will be running for another four hours and it would take ages to get back into the Solent against it. We'll all feel much better when we've had a hot drink and something to eat.'

Dick was silent but he didn't have long to consider the options, his train of thought was interrupted by Teddy lurching across the cockpit to be sick over the lee rail.

'That's the way', said Diana encouragingly, 'You'll soon feel better now.'

Dick was not convinced.

Whose side are you on, are you a stayer or a quitter?   BA

Going back is bad psychology, the kids would dread the next attempt and this situation is going to occur again and again. With no bad weather pending and easier waters ahead press on. Alternatively make for a closer but new destination. Best to put the kids to bed to sleep it off perhaps. Diana should forget the tea and settle for biscuits. I find tea has emetic effects on queasy tummies.   JDS

Yes, Des and Diana are probably right. Keep going. The bumpiest part of the passage is probably behind them and if they can get a hot drink and some food into the crew then morale and enthusiasm should be restored. If not, they will have lost very little by sailing on for another hour or so when the decision can be reconsidered.   BA

Conflicting advice

'. . . *southerly 7, backing southeasterly gale force 8 later.'* I missed the rest of the forecast as I contemplated the reality of our situation, except to hear Royal Sovereign telling of a southerly 6. We were 5 miles south of Brighton, our home port and returning home after our first cross-Channel crossing on *Lynx*, our two year-old French 28ft cruiser racer, a dream to sail in light airs but decidedly lively in the present conditions. It is bad for morale to imagine the worst but having more than once stood at the end of the marina breakwater and witnessed the power of an onshore gale and the maelstrom it created off the entrance as the reflected waves met and amplified the onshore swell I was left with serious doubts as to whether we should, in view of the forecast, even attempt the approach. What I needed was advice on current conditions. I reached for the hand mike of the VHF set.

'Solent Coastguard, this is *Lynx*, over.' After the preamble came back the message. '*Lynx*, this is Solent Coastguard. We had a call from an inshore fishing boat a couple of hours ago just off Brighton. He reported heavy seas in the approaches to the marina. He was going in to refuel but as we haven't heard back from him we can't give you any more information. Suggest you call Brighton Marina for an on the spot report, though if conditions get worse you might consider an alternative destination. Over.' 'Solent Coastguard, this is *Lynx*. Thanks for the advice. Out.' Alternative destination . . . if it really started to blow that meant the Solent, a good 40 miles away to the west. If the forecast was right the full gale could be on us by the time we arrived, let alone the inconvenience of trekking back to Brighton to pick up the car. I called Brighton Marina.

The Harbourmaster was reassuring. 'We've got about 25 knots from the south here,' he came back. 'I can't see the entrance from here but I doubt if it'll give you any real problems – might just be a bit bouncy for the last quarter mile or so. A small fishing boat came in a while back and he didn't report any problems, over.' I breathed a sigh of relief as *Lynx* picked up another following sea and surfed down its face at 9 knots. The radio crackled into life again.

'*Lynx* this is *Girl Stella*. Heard you talking to the Harbourmaster just now – we're the fishing boat he was talking about. I wouldn't try it if I was you, it's bloody rough just off the entrance. We dipped our gunwales a couple of times and shipped a fair amount of water. I'm staying put here – half my party walked off when we arrived, they'd had enough, over.' I thanked him and returned to my dilemma.

Whose advice would you take, and why? And what would you do now?   AB

It is always a dangerous proposition to seek advice about sea conditions over the radio because the quality and relevance of the answer you receive may be distinctly dubious.

Probably the best available help of this is an unemotional statement from a professional observer who is actually on the spot. The Coastguard at the Needles, for example, could see the conditions directly beneath his observation post and his report would, therefore, be reasonably accurate. To request this information from such a source is perfectly reasonable. What is not fair is to ask the observer whether or not you should attempt to pass his stretch of sea. He doesn't know you, he doesn't know your boat, and he cannot tell what changes may occur in the hour or so it will take you to get there.

Our friend is in an understandable quandary. He wants information so

he calls the nearest Coastguard radio station which, as it happens, is miles from the place in which he is interested. The Coastguard does all he can, which is to relay someone else's report, but he goes one step further and, by implication, advises our man that the entrance could by now have become dangerous.

The Harbourmaster's opinion doesn't sound a lot of use. He hasn't even been out to look, which is a pity, because not only is he the man on the spot, but he also knows the place well and could possibly offer a useful opinion on the viability of an approach. Even then, however, it would be unwise to accept his verdict as gospel. After all, we know nothing about him. Has he ever sailed a light boat like Lynx? Perhaps he was a deep-sea fisherman before he took up his present job, or maybe he has never been to sea in his life. We don't know. We would be grateful for his statement about sea state, had he but made one, but that is all. His comments about the fishing boat are of only marginal relevance.

We do know, though, that Girl Stella's master is a practising seaman and that he has recently negotiated the entrance. He has advised us gratuitously that conditions are very bad for his boat. They are probably worse by now; we are aware that the place can be a maelstrom in an onshore gale and we also should have enough experience of Lynx to rate her lower in the 'sea kindliness stakes' than an MFV.

If the skipper is going to listen to anyone, it had better be to Girl Stella, who is advising prudence in circumstances which may well be dangerous. Her call adds up to advice which, once sought, should be taken.

It's tough, but Brighton's not on.

The Solent doesn't sound too attractive either. It will be safe enough if the gale arrives early, but remember, it isn't forecast to pipe up until later, which is at least 12 hours on from now. Although The Solent is downwind, it's an awfully long way, and involves all the logistical aggravations the skipper is concerned about.

How about Newhaven? It's only a few miles further east, and with its fine breakwater, it should pose no desperate problems in the force 6 to 7 that seems most likely to be served up. Even if the wind did blow up to force 8, the entrance should still be possible because it is wide enough to accommodate a yacht whose worst wickedness might be a broach in the steep waves of the approach. However, in all probability, the conditions will still be well short of such unpleasantness by the time the boat arrives.

Newhaven for me. Let's crack on sail and get in as soon as we can! TC

I agree with Tom that Newhaven might be an alternative though in strong onshore winds can also be difficult in the approaches. He did, though, miss a couple of clues which for me make the picture add up to Brighton as first choice.

First, though, the quality of advice. The Coastguard sitting in his office many miles away might have the information at his fingertips but as he's not on the spot can't advise. The Harbourmaster knows the entrance and as no doubt he too will have witnessed boats entering in strong conditions can make a pretty shrewd guess at conditions which are likely to be fairly accurate. *Girl Stella* has just come through and so his advice should be listened to carefully. The first question I would want to ask myself – and him if still in radio contact – is just what sort of boat is he? The clues to that were when he said 'we dipped our gunwales a couple of times and shipped a fair amount of water' and 'half my party walked off when we arrived'. Perhaps it was too obscure to pick up but the impression it was intended to give was that *Girl Stella* is a small open angling boat out on a day trip. *Lynx*, despite being a light cruiser racer should fare very much better in the approaches.

Remember that the wind is still in the south and *Lynx* less than an hour's sailing time away, during which conditions are unlikely to deteriorate significantly. The worst conditions off Brighton occur with a south easterly. In this situation I would at least close to within half a mile of the marina to have a look at sea conditions before making the final decision. If still in doubt then it's time to head for Newhaven, otherwise batten down the hatches, harness and clip on all crew, issue lifejackets, start the engine and reduce sail to small and controllable headsail alone and go for it. AB

The power to hold

One of the great delights of buying a new boat is the planning and purchasing of equipment. The purchase of our new 36-footer was for us the culmination of several years of planning. She was solid, if a bit staid compared with many lightweights of similar size and was to be a little more to us than just another cruising boat. We planned, after two or three years home based cruising, to take early retirement and head for the sun, initially the Mediterranean and then across the Atlantic and after that, who knows. The crew for the most part would be just the two of us, with family and friends joining us en route from time to time. But as far as equipment priorities were concerned, they had to be designed around two fit but not particularly agile 55-year-olds.

Our previous boats had all been secondhand and with them we had inherited a hotch potch of gear and had rarely been afforded the luxury to buy anything from new. Now it seemed that almost every post brought another carton, another pile of polystyrene packing to be dispensed with and another piece of gear to be carefully stored in the spare bedroom. But there was one vital piece of gear we had debated long and hard: the main, bower anchor. The kedge was already decided, a 25lb Danforth inherited from the previous boat. The new boat was to be fitted with a windlass but, with a back that sometimes gave trouble, I was still concerned about having to handle on a day to day basis, what I, ideally, would have liked, a 35lb CQR with $\frac{3}{8}$in chain cable — at least 60 metres of it. I was equally concerned about the possibility of dragging around every harbour we visited.

One solution by the builder. Go for the Bruce anchor, he suggested. It holds so well you'll only need a 15kg anchor with 10 metres of $\frac{3}{8}$in chain and make up the rest of the cable with Anchorplait. What would be your choice?   AB

There is only one criteria in choosing an anchor, how well will it hold? One day he will be anchoring in coral, sand, mud, rock, lava, shell, marl and the rest of the list on Chart 5011. The Bruce may be an excellent burying-type anchor but he already has a Danforth (albeit too light so get a bigger one) so why not make the second anchor a whacking great rock-holding fisherman however awkward it may be? You don't choose an expensive oil painting to cover a damp patch on the wall. JDS

As a kedge that 25lb Danforth may be fine. Perhaps it would also suffice as a 'lunch hook' when you are anchoring for a couple of hours in settled weather but for a 36-foot boat it is patently too light for the working bower anchor. When long distance cruising your ground tackle is very often your lifeline and probably the best insurance you can buy so it doesn't pay to skimp on it.

I like Des' suggestion of a whacking great Fisherman as a back-up. It will probably live in the bilges earning its keep as ballast for most of the time but there will be the occasion when you want every bit of ground tackle out when it will be worth its awkward weight in gold.

But Danforth vs Bruce vs CQR? The Danforth, although one of the best anchors in a straight line pull (hence its use as a kedge) tends to break out and drag before re-bedding if a boat veers at anchor. The Bruce and the CQR both 'carve' their way round and stay embedded in this situation. And I certainly wouldn't skimp on weight by going for the lighter Bruce and less chain, whatever the claims made about the anchor. Weight is one of the prime factors in anchor holding power. No I would opt for the 35lb CQR with its $\frac{3}{8}$in chain cable and then look at ways of making handling as easy as possible. You already have a windlass so why not design and have built a bow roller that will allow the anchor to self stow? You might not keep it there on passage but on shorter trips between anchorages it won't cause any problems.

In 36 feet of boat there should be room for three anchors and although for UK coastal cruising it would be overkill, for the type of sailing planned my inventory for a boat of this size would be: kedge — 25lb Danforth; bower — 35lb CQR; 'storm' anchor — 60lb Fisherman.   AB

Thick thinking

The visibility had been deteriorating as we crossed Poole Bay, though with the aid of the Decca we had been able to find the North Channel, sailed past Hurst Castle and were now off Yarmouth headed for Cowes, under power as the wind had died to nothing as we entered the Solent. As we passed the first of the large mooring buoys the Decca, for reasons best known to itself, produced a few bleeps, a string of hieroglyphics and refused to answer any commands — just like some of my junior crew members, I thought as I went on deck to review the situation.

Visibility was down to a couple of hundred yards so I decided we could continue, buoy hopping along the Island shore and so keeping out of the main channel and away from dangers of shipping. With a lookout posted in the bow we easily followed the chain of mooring buoys and set a course for Hamstead Ledge. At the appointed distance run, having allowed for the flood tide, the murky shape of the buoy appeared fine on the port bow and gracefully accepting the praise from the crew I altered course slightly for the next target, Salt Mead buoy just over two miles distant.

Again my luck held with praise now approaching something nearer disbelief as another minor course change pointed the bows in the direction of Gurnard Ledge, less than two miles away. With that one under our belts, I thought, we're as good as home and dry. . . .

The fog if anything was now thicker — perhaps 100 yards or less. As the log clicked past 1.8 with no sight of the buoy my credibility was under seige. At 1.9 my whole reputation as a navigator was in question and at 2.0 it was going to take a monumental masterstroke of seamanship and pilotage to restore the slightest vestige of confidence. But what masterstroke? AB

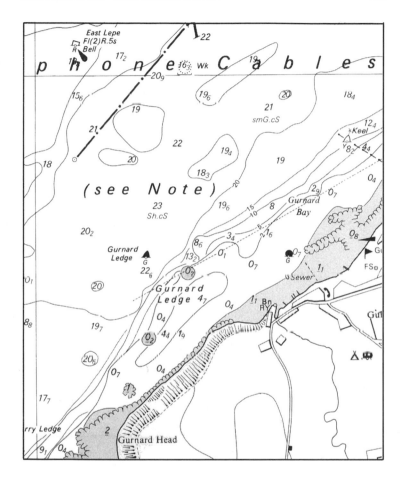

The current may have been dead astern earlier, hence those on-the-nose successes but it may have eddied out of Thorness Bay and set them to seaward of Gurnard Ledge buoy. Gurnard Ledge itself looks very steep-to and easy to find on the echo sounder, I'd say to hell with its buoy and follow the edge of the shallows. The racing buoy 'Keel' is bang on the 5-metre contour and if they miss that they can still follow the edge. JDS

Those contours are so tight and would be so easy to find on the depth sounder that there is little point in going back to find Gurnard Ledge using a square search. A quick hike inshore to pick up the contour, a pair or two of sharp eyes and 'Keel' should appear out of the fog and the skipper's reputation be re-established. Even if they fail to find 'Keel', the skipper could amaze all the disbelievers by sticking to that contour until he reaches Cowes Roads where there are any number of buoys to find close by and then heading carefully into the River and the first land they will see will be the Red Funnel terminal and the Marina, just where they had planned to go.

I found myself doing just this once and off Egypt Point decided to check my position by easing into 3 metres. Suddenly close at hand was the beach and on it a man walking his dog. 'Where are you?' I asked. 'On the beach' came the reply as he was swallowed by the mist.   AB

A need for seamanship

The yacht was a 30ft gaff cutter, a fishing smack lovingly restored, engineless, long of keel and long of bowsprit too, the sort of craft that flies like the wind on a reach but is slow in stays needing careful nursing if she is to be tacked in a jobble of sea. Her owner though loved her faults as much as her virtues and handling her in tricky situations was the stuff of life to him.

He had brought up to anchor just to one side of the river entrance because he couldn't beat in against the ebb and tide-waiting was all part of the game. It was uncomfortable though in a tidal tumble of sea, moreover close to port ran a submerged drain outfall, but with a heavy fisherman anchor well dug home the skipper wasn't perturbed. Like any good single hander with time on his hands he brewed tea and then turned in for a nap until the ebb slackened and he could resume his passage.

A few hours passed, the wind freshened a shade and the tide changed, the jerking and jangling of the gear woke him. It was time to get under way but there was a problem, the smack was now tide-girt, the flood stream was on his port beam and the wind broad on his starboard bow and she lay pinned between the two; no amount of helm applied one way and then the other would bring her head to wind or sheer her to bring the wind on the port bow and he knew that if he got his anchor with the wind on the starboard bow she would bear off straight towards that drain outfall.

A gaff cutter of this breed cannot be tacked instantly like a modern yacht, she has to be sailed off to pick up speed and then brought to head carefully, backing the jib and even reversing the helm to jolly her round and even so she might miss stays and fall off on the old tack again. It was not safe to risk it. Neither could he put a spring on the cable nor could he lead the cable aft and haul in over the stern — not with heavy chain and single handed. He could perhaps have sailed the anchor out, setting the mainsail and sailing ahead until the lead of chain snubbed the smack round onto the port

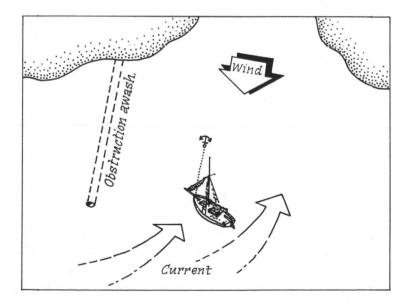

tack, then gathering in chain as she romped over it but he knew it would be a risky and exhausting operation with a dozen things to go wrong. So he did something really quite simple. Do you know what it was?   JDS

———————

The solution to the smacksman's problem is delightful in its purity. He must prepare his main and staysail for hoisting and hoist his jib in stops (ie, fully aloft with sheets bent on and led aft, but furled up to its own luff with lengths of rotten cotton which will break when the sheet is yanked).

Once he is confident that all is prepared, he takes a good look around to ensure that his manoeuvring space will remain free of traffic and then he heaves the smack up to her anchor, weighs, and secures the hook, for quickness under the bobstay below the bowsprit.

As soon as the boat is free of the bottom she will no longer lie 'tide-girt', but will take up her natural angle to the wind. A smack carries her mast and hence most of her windage well forward, somewhat ahead of her centre of lateral resistance. Her maximum draft is aft, at the bottom of her rudder post. The combination of these two factors will ensure that she lies with her head well below square on to the wind, in this case probably starboard side on. (see illustration)

Since, at the moment, she has no sail set, the only way she will tend to move through the water is almost dead downwind. She will not 'sail' far towards the breakwater, if indeed she does at all. It is more likely that the current will carry her, stern first, towards the river mouth, or that the wind and tide will continue to keep her more or less stationary over the ground as her head falls off.

The skipper can take a moment or two now to assess what his boat is doing. He will note a few natural transits along the shore to check the direction of his drift. When he is fully appraised of what is going on, he will break out his jib by hauling aft the port sheet and then sail away to seaward until he has gained sufficient offing to clear any obstructions. As he goes the current will help him to keep off the drain outfall. On his way out he can hoist his staysail, then, when he is content that he is in safe water, he will put his helm down and luff up to hoist his main. The last manoeuvre will present no difficulties for a smack as the little boat will be so steady on the helm that she will remain for a considerable time with the wind forward of the beam before she loses way and stalls. By then, she should be fully clad in her party dress and ready to enjoy that brisk beat up river on a fair tide.

Incidentally, if our friend doesn't like the look of things at any stage of this operation, remember he still has that fine big fisherman anchor slung under the bobstay, ready to be let go on the run at any time. All possibilities are thus covered, and it's time he got under way. TC

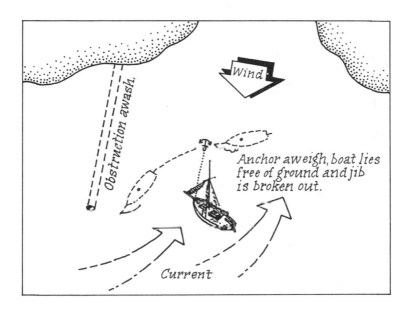

I agree fully with Tom's analysis. Mine ran thus. With wind and current opposing a stalemate situation exists and he took advantage of this. With sails ready to hoist and a single tyer on them he quietly hauled in his anchor up to the stemhead. The smack's bows paid off downwind until she was pointing at the obstruction, but the weight of the tide prevented her from going anywhere. It also gave the skipper steerage way and he was able to turn her to bring the wind on his port quarter, current on the starboard bow, now heading obliquely away from the obstruction. In his own good time he lashed the anchor and set the mainsail scandalised – hauling up the throat and leaving the peak of the gaff swinging loose. This was sail enough to turn her half into the wind and with a lashing on the tiller he completed the hoisting of sail.   JDS

The smart recovery

Margaret and Jane always spent a late season weekend sailing together. They had started to do so many years ago, as a way of sharpening up their sailing skills. Both families owned 25ft cruisers so it didn't much matter whose boat they sailed, the idea was to leave their husbands and children at home so they could spend the whole two days practising different manoeuvres and evolutions.

They had been practising man-overboard recovery manoeuvres for the last half hour. Both were natural helmsmen so they had little difficulty in reaching away from the floating fender which they were using as the 'casualty', tacking and coming back on a close fetch to stop a few feet upwing of the target.

'It's easy under these conditions' said Margaret as she completed an almost perfect approach, 'But I'm never quite sure that opening out so far from the casualty to give yourself room to tack and line up for the approach is a very good idea. If you had to do it at night it would be nice not to have to sail so far away and risk losing sight of your victim.'

'Let's try just heaving to' Jane suggested. "That should stop the boat close enough to the casualty for him to be within heaving line range.'

They tried and it worked well, from any point of sailing, as long as they were quick enough. 'That's fine,' said Jane, 'But if you were a bit slower off the mark, as you might well be if it happened unexpectedly, you might well finish up out of range with the heaving line.'

'The text-book solution is to start the engine, lower the headsail and motor round to approach the casualty from down wind.' Said Margaret. 'Dick and I tried it a couple of weeks ago and it works well. You have to be careful to check for sheets in the water before you put the engine into gear but you never have to open out any distance from your casualty. And it would be even easier for you with your roller furling headsail'.

'You think so?' Answered Jane. 'When did you last try to start our ancient donk? It takes a minute on the heater plugs and five minutes of prayer and libation to the gods before you even get a hopeful splutter out of it. I think we are always going to be safer to rely on our sails. What I would like to try is heaving to, letting the boat fore-reach a little and then seeing if I could gybe round and back to the casualty. I've always thought it should be possible and as well as keeping you close to your victim you should be able to do it without having to wrestle with the headsail sheets, in fact you should hardly have to touch either sheet.'

Jane tried the manoeuvre. How do you think she got on?   BA

––––––

In almost every conceivable situation heaving to is going work from any point of sailing. It will be easiest from a point with the wind forward of the beam which has the added bonus that it may not be necessary to gybe round as the boat will naturally fore reach back towards the victim. A light fin-keeled boat can be sailed out of a hove-to position by gybing if it is necessary. If, however, the boat was on a broad reach or a run when the casualty went over the side it won't quite be a hands off situation. If the mainsheet is left the boat should tack from this point of sailing, but even with the headsail aback she is likely to sail off at some speed in the other direction. Jane will need to sheet in the main as the boat comes round onto the wind which will not only speed up the tack but also prevent a crash gybe when she sails out of the hove to position. The great advantage of heaving to in this situation in a boat of this type is that it slows the boat and brings her under control whilst the helmsman decides on his or her next move. There are no hard and fast rules for man overboard recovery –

the options open to Jane at this stage might be gybing round or she may
choose to lower the headsail onto the foredeck and return to the victim
under more control, especially as she may be overcanvassed for windward
sailing. Or it might be worth spending the five minutes necessary to start
the engine.   AB

—————

The method can work well, given a good helmsman, lots of practice, and fairly flat sea conditions. Otherwise, not recommended and certainly not as a 'standard drill'.   BA

A choice of anchorage

There is nothing very unusual about having to seek out a sheltered haven when bad weather is brewing, usually a spare mooring can be found, a marina berth or a sheltered though inaccessible anchorage way up some muddy creek where one spends a windy night with maybe a bit of fun and games when wind and current conflict. What happens though when the warning is out for winds of storm or even hurricane force?

The 28ft fin keel cruiser was on passage along the coast when her crew heard the storm warning and it was of 'imminent' classification. The nearest shelter which offered was a creek situated within a shallow estuary, a popular although quite small yachting centre and at least partly open to the threatened south to south east storm. There was little hope that the warning might prove an empty threat because all ajacent sea areas carried the same warning, plainly the crew must seek such shelter as they could find and quickly.

By the time they were running into the estuary the wind was south west and force 6, but the tide was flooding and so at least the buoyed channel was relatively quiet with wind and tide together. It was half-flood and already dusk when they found the entrance to the creek and with the wind on their port quarter they went tearing in, feeling some shelter from the land as they entered. So far so good but where could they bring up?

The main body of the creek was densely populated with moored and anchored yachts and with their draft of over five feet the fringing shallows were not much use to them. True there were a couple of gaps between the yachts where settled weather they might have anchored but what other options were there? A VHF call to the marina revealed that the only available berths were in the entrance and rafted up alongside other visitors.

With sails stowed and under engine the skipper stooged around while he thought about it. There was a drying creek on the eastern side, again filled with moored boats and at the head of it there was

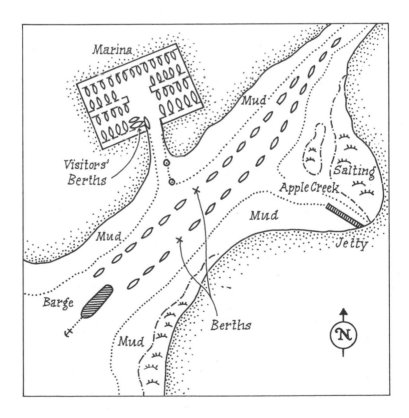

an old jetty which the pilot book said was a quiet berth if you were prepared to dry out alongside. It could only be approached for an hour either side of high water though. High tide was around midnight and it was springs – the jetty might be a possible the skipper thought. Out in the main channel there was another possibility, a large anchored motor barge, could they perhaps stream astern from a warp? It was all extremely worrying, the more so since their ground tackle was none too generous consisting of a 25lb CQR on 40 metres of chain and a further 15 metres of warp and a 15lb kedge on a lighter 20-metre warp. Together though they added up to 40lbs of anchor and a potential 80 metres of warp.

A squall came tearing through the gathering dusk and the wind backed a few degrees. Through the rainy murk the lights of the marina beckoned invitingly. 'Right' said the skipper, 'I've made up my mind. . . .'   JDS

There really is only one choice: to dry out alongside the old jetty but being very careful in the process.

The marina is clearly out of bounds because when the storm arrives from the south east as predicted it will blow straight into the entrance, albeit with little fetch but more than enough to wreak havoc on a raft of yachts alongside. The barge might be tempting because it is obviously on a very heavy mooring. But it is fully exposed to both wind and sea and once the spring ebb has started to run conditions here will not just be dangerous, they will be suicidal, with large breaking seas and the enormous bulk of the barge plunging and veering all over the place.

Drying out is a winner because although the boat will still be exposed to much of the wind, she will, an hour after HW be completely isolated from the potentially damaging seas. The creek is sheltered from the SE so drying out on the muddy bottom and refloating should cause no problems. What might be a problem is the fact that the jetty is described as being old. Will it withstand the strain of the windage of the dried out yacht? Once alongside the leeward side of the jetty and made fast with doubled up warps, her crew must take steps to minimise the chances. If the main

136

anchor is walked ashore to the south east and, if necessary, physically buried the warp can be sweated tight and made fast around the foot of the mast — or if the crew are feeling athletic round the spreaders. The kedge can be deployed in a similar fashion and the main halyard made fast to the strongest convenient point on the quay. As the boat takes the ground at about 0100 every attempt should be made — crew on the side deck and anchor warps hardened in — to heel the boat to windward a few degrees. A watch should be organised with the offwatch crew, if possible, sleeping on the windward side of the boat. After that all the skipper can do is to keep his fingers crossed. He's in the snuggest berth in the harbour and has done all he can to protect his boat. AB

My solution differs from Andrew's, but then it would be wrong to assume there was only one answer to any question of seamanship involving so many variables.

There really isn't a lot of choice, anchoring in the confined spaces available is unthinkable because there will be no room to veer more and more scope (even if they had it to veer) and without doubt there will be threats from nearby yachts and boats adrift. A storm force blow is a solid blast of wind and the anchorage will become a wild melee of drifting craft. Lying astern of the barge would be safe for a while perhaps but it is perilously close to the entrance and scarcely protected, worse though would be when wind and current opposed, nothing could save them then from being smashed against her. Rafting up in the entrance to the marina is also out because even in a comparatively narrow creek a large sea will build up and the yachts would destroy each other. Neither is the jetty a safe option since the storm would probably be at its height before they could even reach it, also the height of tide may be pushed up in a tidal surge and the jetty might be submerged. Undoubtedly too there will be a wind shift at some time, what will that mean?

The only safe place to go is as far up the mud as the state of tide will allow and on the south side of Apple Creek. There the anchors should hold until the ebb leaves her beached, but intact. JDS

Fully fitted rocks

The northern coasts of the Isles of Scilly present an almost unbroken wall of islands and rocks from the diminutive Maiden Bower in the west to White Island and St Martins at the eastern end. Apart from the distinctive islands themselves, the only navigational aid of any kind is the Round Island lighthouse on the distinctive hump backed island of the same name and its long range radio beacon. There are a few leads between the islands offering shelter though none is particularly easy to identify from seaward and all should be entered with caution. Perhaps the best, both in terms of entry and shelter offered, is New Grimsby Sound between the islands of Bryher and Tresco. It is a place to navigate with care, even in daylight and settled weather. We were now approaching this coast just as darkness fell, the islands a low group of anonymous humps and the red eye of Round Island light flashing balefully every 10 seconds, fine on the port bow.

We had left Baltimore on the south west coast of Ireland 36 hours earlier. It had been a hard crossing beating into the strong southeasterly, our intended destination of the Helford River seeming never to come closer. The weather had taken its toll of the crew and we were down to the walking wounded, John, the skipper and an ex-RAF navigator *par excellence*, still suffering from seasickness and myself, fatigued having taken the lion's share of the previous night's watch and been unable to get more than a couple of hours' rest during the day. The other two were totally *hors de combat* below deck and so, in the late afternoon and with a falling wind we had decided to put in to New Grimsby Sound for the night.

Keeping track of our progress had proved little problem thanks to the tireless Decca, though in the last couple of hours it had produced a few anomalous results. Must be getting tired, like me, I thought. It was still overcast and so as the darkness fell we had little to guide us except the Round Island Light and the glowing numbers

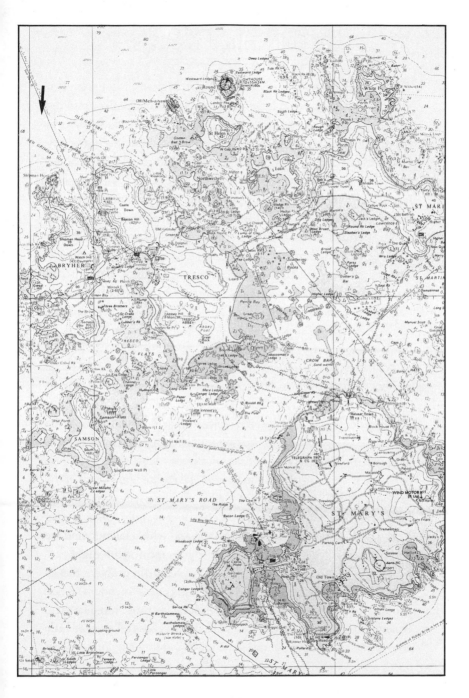

139

on the Decca. A few minutes earlier I had noticed a single, steady white light fine on the starboard bow which disappeared as quickly as it had materialised. We were now, according to both DR and Decca about a mile off, a fact confirmed by a bearing on Round Island. It was decision time. Should we feel our way in, trusting our navigation and eyes? And if so what should be our strategy? Or should we with tired and sick crew stand off for seven or so hours until first light?   AB

I'm not sure whether 'about a mile off' refers to Round Island or the entrance to New Grimsby Sound but I assume it's the latter. In which case that brief glimpse of a white light could have been the Bishop Rock light before it was obscured by the hump of Bryher Island, (they should see its loom anyway). If they stand on, the Peninnis Head light on St Mary's should become visible shining right down New Grimsby Sound on about 160 degrees magnetic, a cross taken on Round Island would also help.

It's not navigation that is the danger but fatigue, both men should check each other's thinking and chartwork.   JDS

Although tired, at least they have quiet weather, good visibility and a first rate navigator. But as Des says they must check and double check their workings.

It was, perhaps, unfair to throw in a wild card. Decca positions around the Isles of Scilly are unreliable owing to what is called 'base line extension'. John should be well aware of this and the fact that the instrument is not to be relied on, especially when closing an unlit rocky shore. There is, however, one completely reliable aid – Round Island. By drawing a line on the chart from the light that clears all dangers by at least two cables they can establish a danger angle. If they then turn to the west, for a mile and then retrace their steps, steering towards Round Island but keeping outside the danger line – checking frequently with the hand bearing compass – they can scan the rocks and islands as they pass looking for that elusive light through New Grimsby Sound. It probably won't be Peninnis Head as that will be obscured by the higher ground of Hugh Town but they should at least see some of the lights of the town and if lucky the riding lights of other yachts at anchor in the sound. Only then and if very sure should they very cautiously head in towards the Sound, with very careful lookout and should soon be rewarded by the silhouette of Cromwell's Castle and Shipman's Head. But if unsure there is only one answer. Stand off 5 miles or so for the night, hove-to so at least some rest is possible before dawn. AB

Hard, fast and thirsty

Captain Cock-up and four of his hearty mates have chartered a 32ft sloop for a weekend of tough sailing and liquid good fellowship. After a heavy Saturday night they were up at 0700 and an hour later were going hard for the entrance to Gasworks Creek 25 miles away where they planned to sink a few pints at the Pipe-fitters Arms before returning with the ebb to Roland Ripoff, the charter operator. The *Naughty Nancy* is due back at 1700.

High Water at Gasworks Creek is at 1130 and closing time is 1400. It is 15 miles from the Pipe-fitters Arms to Roland's place, so they know they are tight for time.

At 1200 the *Naughty Nancy* enters the winding two-mile reach of Gasworks Creek. The wind is dead on the nose. There is water in the centre of the river at all states of the tide and the ebb is not running too hard as yet, but the banks are only marked by withies; all else is mud.

'How about the engine, Captain?' asks Fred, who is feeling exceptionally thirsty.

'Not on your life, Mate,' retorts the Captain, mercilessly. 'We've chartered a sailing boat, not a stink-pot! Whaddaya say, lads?'

There is a rumble of approval from the rest of the hands and as the winches jangle the *Naughty Nancy* into a close-hauled state. Cock-up himself takes the helm and presents his ship at something approaching a useful angle to the force 5 breeze.

'Shake out the reef, now, boys!' he orders, flushed with the delight of entering smooth water. 'We'll stick with the number 2. Another half hour and we'll be tied up.'

Fred is still fighting a rearguard action on behalf of a fast, safe arrival at the watering hole. 'Don't you think this is a waste of drinking time?' he argues. 'And what about Roland Ripoff? If we're late back he'll soak us by the hour for penalty money.'

'Don't you worry, m'son,' reassures the gallant Captain. 'We'll be up there in two shakes. The channel's clearly marked by these withies and the ebb'll swish us back down again in no time once we're tried the beer. . . . Ready about!' With a thunder of canvas and a rattle of winches, the *Naughty Nancy* swings round onto the port tack, heels to her increased press of sail and surges away towards the opposite bank. The creek is now about 150yds wide between the markers.

On this tack they approach the reeds between two withies and just before they reach the imaginary line joining them up, Captain Cock-up heaves the helm down with a cry of 'Lee-ho'. The *Naughty Nancy* comes upright as the headsail sheet is cast off, but instead of swinging smoothly onto the new tack, she glides inexorably to a halt. She hesitates for a moment head to wind, then her bow falls off to starboard, pointing for the bank; she heels over as the wind catches her mainsail and begins to drive further ashore. The headsail thunders and all hands look expectantly at their Captain, except Fred, who looks at his watch.

'Next High Water's midnight, skipper,' he advises, 'that'll be about 12 hours we'll owe Roland Ripoff. Pity we finished the canned beer last night. . . .' he continues, but Captain Cock-up, concerned about the effect of dissent on crew morale, silences him by a gesture with a winch handle.

'We'll get her off, lads!' he growls. 'Don't you listen to Fred.

Now. Here's what we'll do . . .'

Is Cock-up in with a chance on the falling tide? If so, how can he expedite his early release from the mud and make it to the Pipe-fitters for a stiffener before closing time? TC

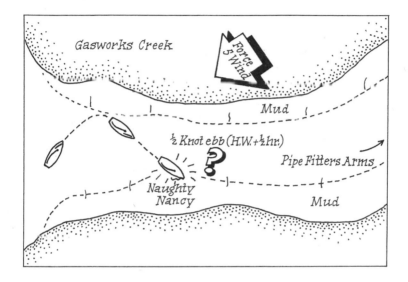

Captain Cock-up has got to act fast. Although the ebb is only slight at the moment as minutes go by it will accelerate and leave them high, dry, beerless and well into their charter penalty clauses. But he has several factors going for him.

But first he must stop the Naughty Nancy from driving herself further onto the mud by freeing off the mainsheet and then use all the weapons at his disposal to get her off. These are the wind, the tide and the engine. He must next get her head through the wind. We have to make a few assumptions about her keel form. Being a charter boat she is likely to be quite modern and most likely a fin keeler. Using the engine and with the rudder hard over to port he won't be able to power off the mud but he will be able to make her pivot on her keel — before doing this he should have sheeted home the genoa so that as the bows go through the wind the sail backs and she effectively fetches up hove to on the starboard tack. His four *hearty crew can now earn their beer money, leaning out to port to heel her and reduce the draught. The mainsail sheeted hard home will do the same. And now, with the tide on her weather bow, the drive from her mainsail and plenty of welly on the throttle she should slip quickly off into deep water.*

Now's the time for Fred to be heeded. If he wants his lunchtime pint Captain Cock-up should lower and stow sail and motor to the Pipe-fitters Arms — and be ready to stand the first round. AB

———

The Captain is right to go for immediate positive action. The vital thing, as Andrew points out, is to get *Naughty Nancy's* head through the wind and the genoa aback on the starboard side. Once this is achieved, the rest should be pure gravy.

The one problem I would foresee is that the windage of the flogging genoa may stop the boat pivotting onto the other tack. If this proves to be the case, the boys should smartly drop the sail on deck and then go and cuddle each other in the pulpit. This will reduce *Nancy's* draft and cut down her forward windage, especially if they sit down as they cuddle. Once the bow is through the wind, the genoa can be rapidly hoisted and brought aback, as specified.

As soon as they're off I'm with Andrew, heeding Fred's advice and demanding that Captain Cock-up buys the drinks. TC